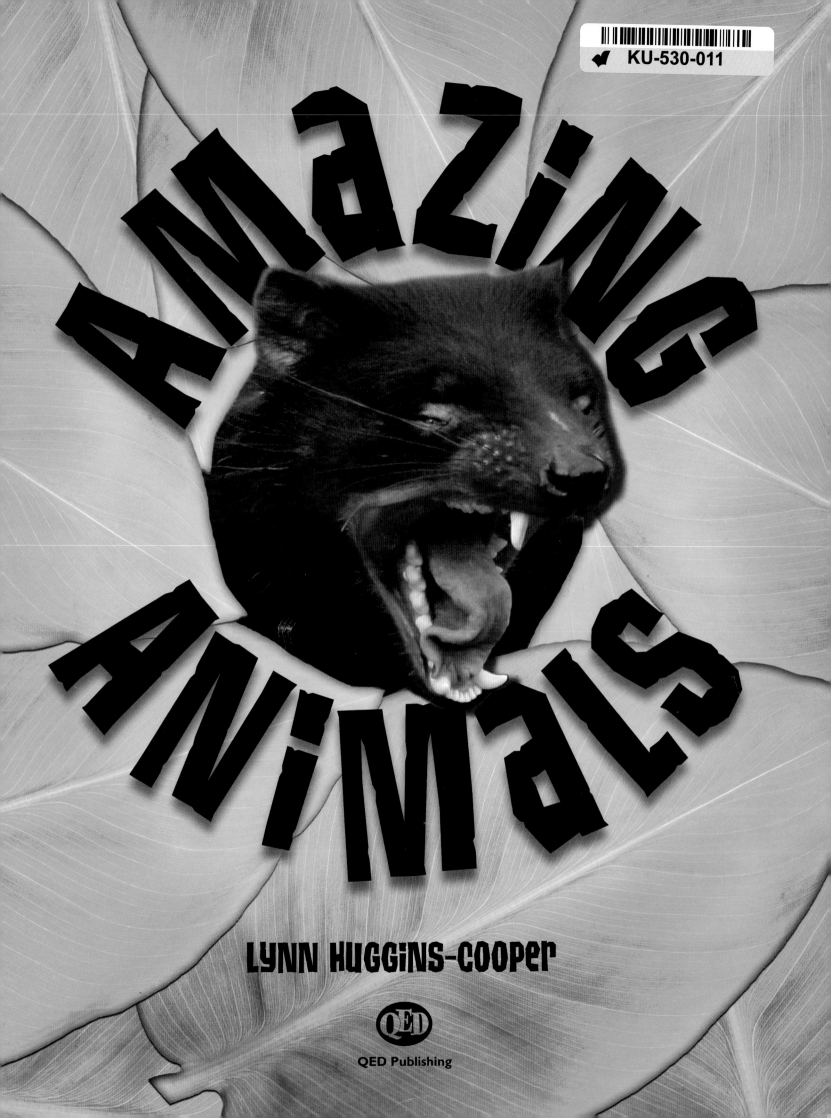

AMAZING ANIMALS

LYNN HUGGINS-COOPER

QED

QED Publishing

Contents

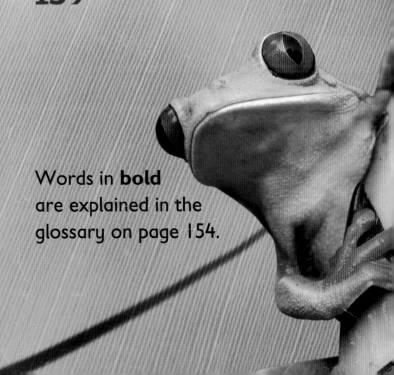

Words in **bold** are explained in the glossary on page 154.

Watch out!

From tropical **rainforests** to dry deserts, from meadows and parks to our own houses, creepy crawlers are everywhere – so watch out!

▲ Weta are large, wingless crickets that live in New Zealand and on the nearby islands.

Different types

Very many of the creepy crawlers we see around us are insects. All insects, such as dragonflies, beetles, wasps and ants, have six legs and three body parts. There are over a million different **species** of insects crawling, flying and creeping across the Earth. Other creepy crawlers include spiders and, in the oceans, **crustaceans** such as crabs and shrimps.

Creepy?

Although many people are scared of insects and other creepy crawlers, they really are amazing creatures worth taking a closer look at. They can survive in the most hostile environments, including places that people cannot live.

◄ Scientists believe that over 90 percent of all the creatures alive today are insects.

Large ancestors

Some creepy crawlers are huge. The Malaysian giant stick insect, for example, grows about as long as a man's arm, and goliath beetles can weigh as much as a family-sized bar of chocolate. But today's creepy crawlers are small compared to creatures from **prehistoric** times. Some 390 million years ago, 2.5-metre-long sea scorpions swam in the oceans and 3-metre-long centipedes scurried through the forests.

▼ *Goliath beetles are probably the largest, heaviest insects in the world. They help keep the Earth clean by eating dead plant material.*

Cool fish

Freaky fish are found everywhere, from the depths of the oceans to muddy river beds. At least 28,000 **species** of fish are known to exist, and new species are being discovered every year.

▲ *Many fish are now protected.* **Aquarium** *fish are bred in captivity rather than being caught in the wild.*

▼ *The great white shark has a terrible reputation for being a* **maneater**, *and has been over-hunted because of this.*

Endangered

In 2007, the World Conservation Union described 1201 species of fish as being threatened with **extinction**. Their list included species such as the Atlantic cod and the great white shark. Fish are at risk because too many are taken from the oceans by fishermen, their habitats are being destroyed by pollution and too many tropical fish are being caught to be sold as pets.

▲ *The whale shark is the world's largest species of fish. It can be up to 14 metres long, which is longer than an average school bus.*

Save our fish

There is a huge variety of life in our lakes, rivers, seas and oceans. Some deep-sea fish produce strange points of light. Some fish are cleverly **camouflaged**, some are extremely poisonous, and there is even a vicious vampire fish that sucks the blood of other living fish. The world is full of freaky fish, and they are all worth protecting.

Freaky flyers

The world is full of amazing birds. They come in all shapes and sizes, from tiny wrens and hummingbirds to huge birds of prey. Birds are not the only animals that fly. Bats and insects fly, too. We will also look at some strange-looking bats.

▼ *While feeding from flowers, hummingbirds hover in mid-air. Most* **species** *do this by flapping their wings about 50 times per second.*

▲ *Many birds carry food to their young in their stomach. They* **regurgitate** *the food for the young to eat.*

All shapes of beaks

Some birds have developed special features and habits for survival. Ducks, for example, have paddle-shaped beaks to help them sieve food from the water. Hummingbirds have long, pointed beaks that they poke deep into flowers so they can drink the **nectar**.

Horrid habits

Birds have many habits that we might think of as unpleasant. These include feeding their young with regurgitated food. Some bats have horrid habits, too. The vampire bat drinks the blood of living creatures. Fruit bats, or flying foxes, like sweet, juicy fruit, just like we do! They can be very large, with a wingspan of 1.5 metres.

▲ *After they feed on fruit, they lick their claws clean.*

Cold blood!

Reptiles include lizards, snakes and crocodiles. **Amphibians** include soft-skinned frogs and salamanders. Both amphibians and reptiles are cold-blooded animals, which means that their body temperature is the same as the temperature of the surrounding air.

▲ *Like modern crocodiles, the **dinosaur T-rex** had sharp teeth for grabbing food.*

Reptiles old and new

Dinosaurs were reptiles that lived millions of years ago. Like modern reptiles, they had no fur and they hatched from eggs. The teeth and skin of some dinosaurs were similar to those of modern alligators, and some dinosaurs may have been as intelligent as crocodiles. Dinosaurs are now **extinct**.

◀ *Many salamanders, such as the Ecuador mushroomtongue salamander, do not have lungs or **gills**. They get the oxygen they need through their skin.*

Amphibians

Amphibians have **adapted** to life in and out of water. They are able to breathe through their skin, although most adult amphibians also have lungs for breathing. When they face a **predator**, many amphibians pretend to be dead, in the hope that the predator will leave them alone. Some amphibians produce **toxins** in their skin that make them taste bad to predators.

◀ *Poison-dart frogs have poisonous skin. Local tribespeople in South America rub the frogs against the skin of young parrots. The poison makes the parrots grow feathers of different colours.*

Really wild!

The animal world is full of amazing creatures. Some look cute, but the sweetest-looking animals may be very fierce. Creatures that look scary may be gentle and shy. Other animals are very colourful and extraordinary-looking, which helps them to survive in their natural environment.

▲ *Weasels are fierce predators. They have beautiful fur like a cat, but you cannot stroke them!*

Bad behaviour?

Animals kill other animals because they need to eat. Sometimes, animals attack people, and we think of this behaviour as vicious. All wild animals can be dangerous. If a man enters a bear's territory, the bear may follow its instincts and attack, just as it would if any other wild animal threatened its territory. Its behaviour is not vicious, it is natural wild animal behaviour.

◀ *Bears will attack if they are surprised, feel threatened or are protecting their territory or* **cubs**.

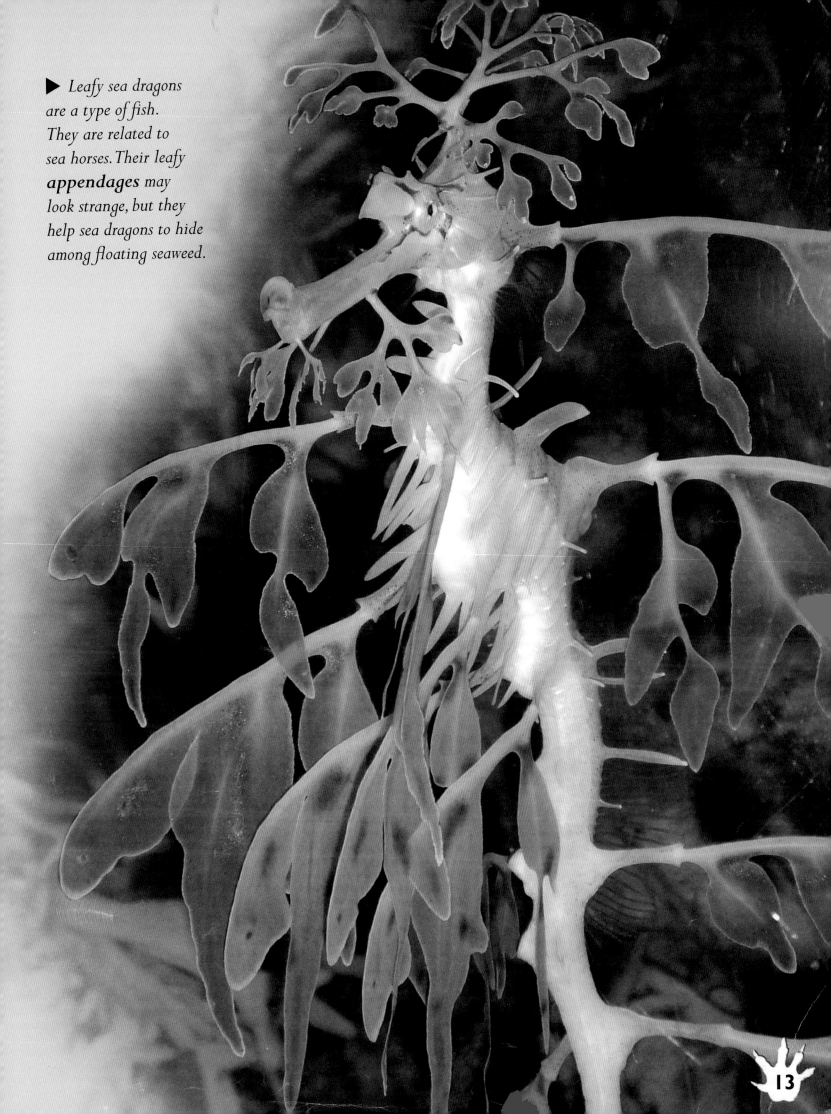

▶ *Leafy sea dragons are a type of fish. They are related to sea horses. Their leafy* **appendages** *may look strange, but they help sea dragons to hide among floating seaweed.*

13

Slippery living

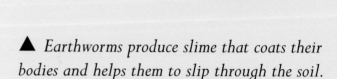

Slimy creatures often make people shudder. But slime comes in very useful for lots of animals. They may use it to help them move, to keep cool and damp, as a defence against **predators** or to protect their eggs.

▶ Earthworms produce slime that coats their bodies and helps them to slip through the soil.

Slime for slipping along

Slime makes it easier for many animals to slip across surfaces or to burrow underground. Some creatures that do not have legs produce slime to help them slide quickly.

*▼ In dry weather, the Australian burrowing frog burrows into the ground and makes itself a slimy **cocoon**. The slime keeps the frog moist. When it rains, the frog climbs out of its burrow.*

Other uses of slime

Some frogs and toads that live in dry, hot places ooze a slimy coating to keep themselves damp during dry periods. A number of salamander **species** produce poisonous slime to stop other creatures from eating them. Some snakes and lizards even use slimy **spittle** to help them to feed. They coat their **prey** in spit to help them swallow. Most **amphibians** lay eggs in water, inside a layer of slimy jelly. The jelly swells in the water and protects the young from cold, diseases and small predators.

Slimy fish

Fish produce slime from **cells** in the outside layer of their skin. The slime prevents many **parasites** from attaching themselves to the scales of the fish. The slime also provides a protective coat over wounds.

▲ *When parrotfish sleep, they cover themselves in a cocoon of slime to stop predators from sniffing them out.*

Smelly animals

Some animals really stink! However, the smells do have a purpose. A stinky smell can make an animal more attractive to its mate, or it may keep predators at a safe distance.

▲ *Moonrats have a long, sensitive nose for detecting smells. They hiss at other moonrats on their territory.*

Moonrats

Moonrats live in the rainforests and **mangrove swamps** of Sumatra, Borneo and the Malay Peninsula. They mark their **den** with a liquid that smells like rotting onions or garlic. The smell warns other moonrats and predators to stay away from their territory.

Polecats

Polecats live in woodland areas of Europe, Asia and North Africa. They mark their territories with a foul-smelling liquid, made in **glands** at the base of the tail. People once used the word 'polecat' to describe someone with a character as foul as the polecat's smell.

◄ *Polecats mostly hunt at night. Their keen sense of smell helps them to detect rabbits, rats, birds, snakes, frogs and fish.*

Musk ox

The musk ox lives in cold regions, in Greenland and northern Canada. Males, called bulls, produce a strong-smelling liquid in glands just under their eyes. To release the smell, the bull rubs its face on trees and bushes. The smell attracts females, who can detect it from a long way off.

▶ *The musk ox has long hair with a thick layer of wool underneath.*

Terrors of the deep

The ocean depths are home to some very strange fish. Some have terrifying teeth. Others have small, light-producing cells on their bodies that attract **prey**.

▲ *At night, marine hatchetfish rise to a depth of 50 metres below the surface to feed. They return to deeper water before dawn.*

Marine hatchetfish

Marine hatchetfish live at depths of 200 to 6000 metres in the Atlantic, Pacific and Indian oceans. Small cells, called **photophores**, on the undersides of their bodies, give off tiny spots of light that point downwards. These lights may attract mates. They may also lure prey from below.

Spookfish

Some types of spookfish are also known as barreleyes because they have tube-shaped eyes. Barreleyes live deep in the Atlantic, Pacific and Indian oceans, at depths of 400 to 2500 metres. Their sensitive eyes point upwards and are able to detect **predators** swimming in the dim water above them.

◄ *The bones of a barreleye's skull are so thin that you can see its brain between its eyes.*

▶ *The barbeled dragonfish is a fierce predator in spite of its small size — about 15 centimetres long.*

Barbeled dragonfish

Barbeled dragonfish live in **tropical** oceans at depths of up to 1500 metres. The female has a long **barbel** under its lower jaw that it waves backwards and forwards to attract prey. The barbel has a light-producing **organ** at the tip, and the fish can flash the light on and off. As soon as prey draws near, the dragonfish snaps it up with its ferocious jaws.

Foul fact!

The young of some dragonfishes have eyes on the end of long stalks, unlike their parents.

Funky frogs

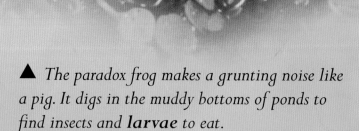

Frogs live all over the world, except in icy **Antarctica**. Most **species** live in **tropical** countries with warm, damp climates, but some prefer hot deserts. Some frogs have developed unusual ways of protecting their young.

▼ *This frog is not shown life-sized here. At only 25 millimetres long, the pouched frog is about the size of a cherry.*

▲ *The paradox frog makes a grunting noise like a pig. It digs in the muddy bottoms of ponds to find insects and **larvae** to eat.*

Paradox frog

The paradox frog lives in ponds and lakes in South America and on the Caribbean island of Trinidad. Adult paradox frogs are about 6 centimetres long, but their **tadpoles** are much larger, at up to 22 centimetres long. As the tadpoles develop into adults, they shrink.

Pouched frog

The pouched frog lives in a small area of central-eastern Australia. Unusually, the female lays a pile of eggs in damp soil rather than in water. As the eggs hatch into tiny, white tadpoles, the male hops into the middle of the pile, and the tadpoles wriggle into two pouches just above his back legs. The tadpoles stay in his pouches until they are ready to emerge as fully formed, small frogs.

Lake Titicaca frog

The Lake Titicaca frog lives only in Lake Titicaca in South America. Lake Titicaca is 3812 metres above sea level. At this **altitude**, the air is very thin – it has less oxygen than places nearer sea level. To cope with these conditions, the Lake Titicaca frog has developed saggy skin with many folds. The frog soaks up oxygen through its skin and the extra skin increases the amount of oxygen that it can absorb.

▼ *The Lake Titicaca frog can survive underwater as it absorbs oxygen from the water through its skin. It sometimes does strange 'press-ups' underwater that disturb the water and make more oxygen flow.*

Foul feeders

Birds, such as vultures, eat **carrion**. Turkey vultures sometimes regurgitate what they have eaten because the smell of rotting food puts off **predators**. Other birds regurgitate food to feed their young.

▲ *The hoatzin cannot fly well. It spends a lot of time perching as it digests its meal, making it vulnerable to predators, such as monkeys.*

Hoatzin

The hoatzin, or 'stinky cowbird', is a South American cuckoo that smells of cow manure! It uses **bacteria** to **ferment** plant materials in the front part of its gut. This helps the bird to digest its food. The smell is strong enough to put off predators.

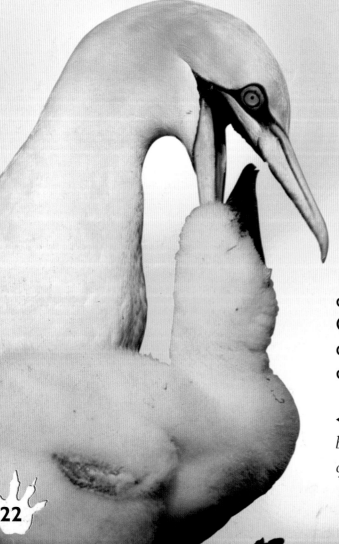

Gannets

Gannets are seabirds. They eat large amounts of fish, such as pilchards, anchovies and squid. Gannets often regurgitate the contents of their stomach if they are disturbed or alarmed.

◀ *A baby gannet will tap its mother's beak to get her to regurgitate a meal of partially digested fish.*

Vultures

Vultures are **scavengers** — they eat the remains of dead animals that have been killed by predators, such as lions. Groups of vultures fly in circles above a dying animal, knowing that they will soon have a feast. Vultures have amazingly strong acid in their stomach to help them digest food. Some vultures can even digest bones.

Foul fact!

Most vultures have a bald head. Feathers would be difficult to keep clean as the birds feed on carcasses.

◀ *Different species of vulture feed on the same carcass at different times. White-headed vultures rip open the carcass, white-backed vultures (shown here) eat the insides, and lappet-faced vultures finish off the tough leftovers.*

Sticky slugs

Slug slime helps prevent slugs from drying out. It also makes travelling across the ground easier and allows slugs to stick to steep surfaces. The slime from one slug even makes predators' tongues go numb, which protects the slug from attack.

▼ *Leopard slug slime, like the slime of other slugs, becomes more sticky if it gets wet, so it is better to rub off the slime rather than to try and wash it off.*

▲ *The black slug covers itself in a thick foul-tasting mucus which protects it against predators and keeps it moist.*

Black slug

The black slug can come in a variety of different colours, including brown and white. It is often active in the daytime, when other slugs are hiding from the sun under rocks and leaves. Gardeners see more of this slug than other slugs and tend to think it does more damage than other species. However, the black slug mainly eats dead and rotting plants.

Leopard slug

The leopard slug is common in Great Britain and Ireland. It now also lives along the east and west coasts of North America, which it reached by crawling ashore from European ships that travelled there. The leopard slug is well **camouflaged** with spots and stripes. It can grow up to 20 centimetres long – the length of a man's hand.

Slugs and snails are gastropods, which means 'stomach foot'. They move along on a single, squashy foot.

Grey field slug

The grey field slug is fairly small, at just 3 centimetres long, but is one of the most serious slug pests. It spends its life above ground feeding on plants, unlike most slugs, which spend most of their time in the earth. Like other slugs, it eats twice its body weight every day. It also breeds quickly, particularly when the weather is warm and damp.

▶ *The grey field slug can munch its way through whole fields of crops. Its slime is usually clear, but when the slug is disturbed the slime becomes thick, white and sticky.*

Spooky spiders

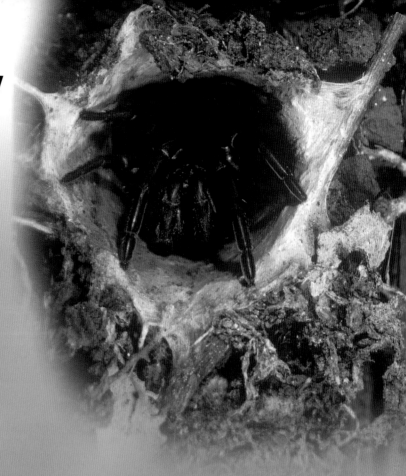

Spiders are scary to millions of people, perhaps because they can scuttle so fast. Some spiders leap out and ambush their victims. Others inject poison when they bite.

▲ *A funnel web spider sits at the entrance to its burrow, ready to pounce on its* **prey**.

Tarantulas

There are an incredible 800 to 1000 species of tarantulas living in warm parts of the world, such as Africa, southern Europe, Australia, South America and Asia. Some live in deserts, others prefer rainforests. They eat insects, other spiders, small **reptiles**, frogs and even small birds.

Funnel web spiders

Funnel web spiders live in Australia. They have sharp, strong **fangs** that they use to inject **venom** into their prey, which includes beetles and skinks. Their venomous bites can cause serious illness or death in humans, but cats and dogs are more resistant to the poison.

◀ *Although tarantulas are venomous, no-one is known to have died as a result of a tarantula bite.*

▼ *The female golden orb web spider strings her webs between trees. The webs are strong enough to snare birds, although the birds are not eaten by the spider.*

Golden orb web spiders

Golden orb web spiders live in Africa and Australia. The spiders are small, but their webs can be up to 2 metres wide, and can last for several years. The silk is so strong that it has been used in the South Pacific to make fishing nets. Some people have used the webs to cover wounds and stop them bleeding.

Foul fact!

'Golden' in the golden orb web spider's name describes the colour of the web, rather than the spider itself.

Clever tricks

Some fish perform amazing tricks to keep themselves safe from predators and to catch their prey.

Porcupine pufferfish

The porcupine pufferfish eats small creatures and shellfish that it finds on the ocean floor. Feelers hanging down from its nostrils help it to find food, such as crabs, shellfish and sea urchins. When it finds its prey, it crushes it in its beaklike mouth.

▲ *The royal gramma lives among the coral reefs of the Caribbean Sea, around the Bahamas and as far north as Florida.*

Royal gramma

The royal gramma, also called the fairy basslet, is half purple and half yellow. Its attractive colours make it a popular aquarium fish. The most unusual thing about this fish is that all the young are born as females. The females can change to become males if there are not enough males about.

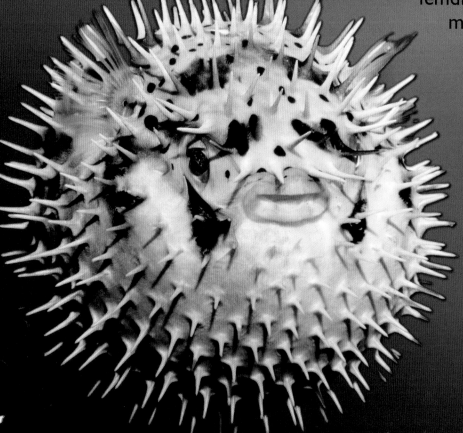

◀ *When the porcupine pufferfish is alarmed, it **inflates** itself by swallowing water. Its spines, which usually lie flat, stick out. This helps it to scare away predators.*

▶ The male Siamese fighting fish looks after his bubble nest. If any eggs fall out of the nest, he spits them back.

Siamese fighting fish

Siamese fighting fish are found in **rice paddies**, ponds and streams in Thailand, Indonesia, Malaysia, Vietnam and China. As the female lays her eggs, the male fish catches them in his mouth and spits them into a nest of bubbles that he has made.

Foul fact!

A male Siamese fighting fish is aggressive towards other males, and will even attack its own reflection in a mirror.

Foul flies

Flies can be very annoying, buzzing around our heads and landing on our food. If, however, you take a closer look, you will see that they are truly amazing flyers.

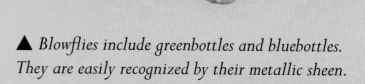

▲ *Blowflies include greenbottles and bluebottles. They are easily recognized by their metallic sheen.*

Snakeflies

There are about 200 different snakefly species. Snakeflies live in North America, Europe and central Asia. They eat small prey, such as aphids and young caterpillars. The female lays her eggs under bark. The eggs hatch into **larvae** that live under bark and in **leaf litter**.

▼ *An adult snakefly can lift its head high above the rest of its body, in a similar way to an attacking snake.*

Blowflies

Female blowflies lay eggs on meat or on the open wounds of injured animals, such as sheep. A female blowfly can lay up to 2000 eggs in her lifetime. Only eight hours after being laid, the eggs hatch into maggots, which feed on the meat.

Foul fact!

Snakeflies are one of only two groups of insects that can run backwards at full speed.

Robber flies

Robber flies are often found in dry, sandy places. They are aggressive hunters, preying on spiders, beetles, other flies, butterflies, bees and other flying insects. A robber fly catches its prey in the air. It has a sharp point on its head that it uses to pierce the flesh of its prey. Then it injects **saliva** into the other creature. The saliva paralyzes the prey, so that the robber fly can suck out its juices.

▶ *A robber fly has a thick, bristly moustache that helps to protect its face from prey struggling to escape.*

Slimy snails

Snails are found all over the world, in gardens, ponds, on the seashore, in the woods – everywhere! Their shells give them protection from predators and the drying effects of the wind and sun.

▼ *A baboon inspects a giant African land snail. The largest giant African land snail ever found was 37.5 centimetres long and weighed nearly 2 kilograms.*

▶ *Periwinkles are a favourite food of many seabirds. Some people also like to eat them, as the snails are high in **protein** and low in fat.*

Periwinkles

Periwinkles are snails that live on the seashore. At low tide the periwinkle is exposed to the air. To stop itself from drying out, it uses slime to seal the gap between its shell and the plant or rock it is on. This allows it to stay moist until the sea covers it again.

Giant African land snails

There are three species of giant African land snail. They are found in many warm, **tropical** countries. One species, the East African land snail, lives in Kenya and Tanzania, but is also found in south and east Asia, the Caribbean and many Pacific islands. It eats rotting plants, fruit and vegetables, as well as bones and shells that provide **calcium** to make its own shell strong.

Garden snails are so good at digesting cellulose that they even eat damp paper and cardboard.

Brown garden snail

The brown garden snail is common in Britain and Europe. It is found in gardens, parks, forests and even sand dunes. It feeds on rotting plants, **algae**, **fungi** and **lichen**. It is most active in wet weather and at night. If the weather gets too dry, the snail goes into its shell and seals the entrance. It can survive like this for months without water.

▶ *The brown garden snail has a long tongue, called a* **radula**, *covered in horny teeth. It eats by scraping the radula over food, such as lichen.*

Putrid pellets

Many larger birds, such as owls and birds of prey, hunt small animals and birds. They gulp down their prey whole, but cannot digest bones, feathers or fur. These tough parts form pellets that the birds cough up and leave on the forest floor.

Peregrine falcon

The peregrine falcon hunts other birds. It flies over open ground and hedges to flush out its prey, and then swoops. Having caught a bird, the falcon takes it to a 'plucking post', such as a tree stump, and pulls out the bird's feathers before eating the rest.

▼ *The peregrine falcon eats the head, feet, intestines and most of the bones of its prey.*

Foul fact!

A peregrine falcon punches its prey in mid-air with a clenched foot, then turns to catch the prey as it falls.

Red-tailed hawk

The red-tailed hawk eats mice, squirrels, rabbits and other birds. It watches for prey from a perch, and then swoops down, sometimes flying low and chasing its **quarry** across the ground. The red-tailed hawk eats all of its prey, regurgitating the parts that it cannot digest in small pellets.

◄ *The red-tailed hawk has long, broad wings which help it soar through the air.*

Owls

Part of an owl's stomach is called the **gizzard**. Here, the fur, bones and other indigestible parts of its prey are squashed into a pellet. The stored pellet stops the owl from feeding again, so the owl coughs up or regurgitates the pellet.

▶ *If you pull an owl's pellet apart, you can see the tiny bones of the bird's prey.*

Beastly biters

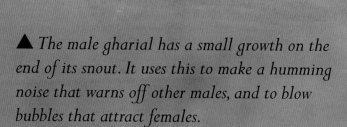

Alligators, crocodiles and the Indian gharial have lots of terrifying teeth. They grow replacements if their teeth are lost or broken.

Alligators

There are two species of alligator – the huge American alligator and the much smaller Chinese alligator, which is almost extinct. Alligators live in swamps, freshwater ponds, rivers and **wetlands**. They pounce on their prey, which include reptiles, **mammals** and birds, if they get too close.

▼ *An alligator kills its prey, such as this brown pelican, by gripping it and pulling it underwater until it drowns.*

▲ *The male gharial has a small growth on the end of its snout. It uses this to make a humming noise that warns off other males, and to blow bubbles that attract females.*

Indian gharial

The Indian gharial lives in small numbers in the rivers of north-east India, Bangladesh, Nepal and Bhutan. Large males can reach almost 6 metres long. The gharial is clumsy on land, but is very quick in the water. It catches small fish and other creatures by snapping its jaws as it sweeps its head from side to side.

Caimans

Caimans are the largest predators in South America's **Amazon basin**. They can reach 4 to 5 metres long – the length of an average estate car. Caimans eat fish, including piranhas, which are aggressive meat eaters themselves. They also eat turtles, birds, deer, **tapirs** and even **anacondas**.

▼ *An adult caiman swallows a large fish whole. The acid in the caiman's stomach is so strong that it can digest every part of its prey, including bones and tough skin.*

Foul fact!

During the dry season, caimans crowding together in small ponds have been known to eat each other.

37

Animal Stickers

Some animals are sticky and others can stick to things using **suction**. Long, sticky tongues allow some animals to catch their food. Others use suction pads to move around or cling onto branches or rocks.

▲ When alarmed by a predator, the black-spotted sticky frog puffs itself up and turns its back to the predator, showing off two large spots. To the predator, this view looks like a snake's head.

Black-spotted sticky frog

The black-spotted sticky frog lives in the rainforests of South East Asia. At night, it hunts for insects on the forest floor. The frog releases a sticky slime when it is threatened, making it an unpleasant meal for predators.

Numbat

The numbat, or banded anteater, lives in the forests of south-west Australia. It uses its nose to track down **termite mounds**. When it finds one, the numbat pokes its long, sticky tongue into holes in the mound. The termites stick to the tongue and the numbat has a feast!

◄ The numbat eats about 20,000 termites every day.

Crown-of-thorns starfish

The crown-of-thorns starfish lives in warm seas and feeds on coral. Thousands of tiny tube feet underneath its arms help the starfish to move around. The feet have suction cups that allow the starfish to cling onto rocks.

▼ *The crown-of-thorns starfish is covered in long, poisonous spines.*

Foul fact!

The crown-of-thorns starfish is usually about the size of a dinner plate, but can be as big as a car tyre.

Putrid parasites

Parasites are creatures that live by feeding off another living creature, called the host. They are among the creepiest of creepy crawlers.

▼ *The **eyestalks** of this snail are infected with parasitic flatworms. The flatworms wriggle inside the eyestalks, and look to a bird like tasty caterpillars.*

▲ *An aphid parasite searches for aphids using the long **antennae** on its head.*

Aphid parasites

Aphid parasites are tiny black wasps. An adult lays its egg inside an aphid. The egg hatches and the parasite develops into an adult wasp inside the aphid's body. The wasp leaves its host by cutting a circular hole in the aphid and flying out.

Parasitic flatworms

One species of parasitic flatworm preys on birds. It starts life as an egg, found in a bird's droppings. A snail slithers along and eats the bird's droppings, including the flatworm's egg. The egg hatches into a flatworm inside the snail. The flatworm moves through the snail, and settles in one of its eyestalks. A bird eats the snail, and the flatworm ends up inside the bird's stomach, where it lays its eggs. The flatworm's eggs pass out in the bird's droppings, and the cycle begins again.

Ichneumon wasps are sometimes called 'scorpion wasps', due to their long, curved bodies that end in a 'sting'.

Ichneumon wasps

There are thousands of species of ichneumon wasps. Females have a long tube, called an ovipositor, at the end of their body, which they use to inject their eggs into other animals. Some species inject their eggs into caterpillars. When the eggs hatch into larvae, the caterpillars split open and die.

◄ *Some species of ichneumon wasps lay their eggs under tree bark close to wood wasp larvae that are living in the wood. They lay their eggs in tunnels made by the larvae.*

41

Wriggly worms

Have you ever held a worm? If you have, you'll know exactly how slimy these wriggly creatures can be. Worms do not just live in soil. They also live in the sea and along the shoreline.

Foul fact!

The velvet worm can shoot its slime up to a distance of 30 centimetres.

▲ *The velvet worm squirts slime at predators in self-defence as well as to catch prey.*

Velvet worms

Velvet worms live in **leaf litter** and rotten logs. They can capture animals, such as spiders, that are several times their own size. To do this, the velvet worm squirts sticky slime at its prey. The prey gets tangled in the slime and is unable to escape. The velvet worm then bites off parts of the captured animal and dribbles acid **saliva** on the parts to make them mushy. It then sucks the mush up into its mouth.

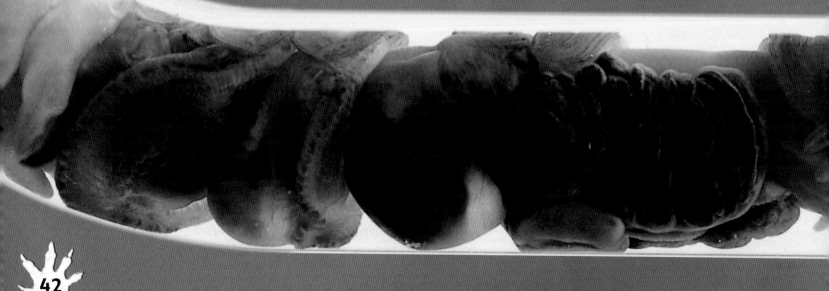

Ragworms

Ragworms are marine worms, which means they live in the sea. They build U- or J-shaped burrows in the sand or mud. The burrows are generally about 20 to 40 centimetres long. The ragworm spins a sticky 'web' across its burrow to catch tiny floating plants called **phytoplankton** from the water. It then eats the web and anything caught in it.

Parchment worm

The parchment worm lives on the coast of Britain in a tube that it **secretes** in the sand. Its body has three parts. The front part contains **glands** that secrete the tube it lives in. The middle part has winglike lobes that secrete the **mucus** that it uses to catch food particles from the water. The last part of its body is made up of lots of small segments.

▲ *Ragworms look as if they have frilly edges. These frills are actually paddles that they use to swim, crawl and burrow.*

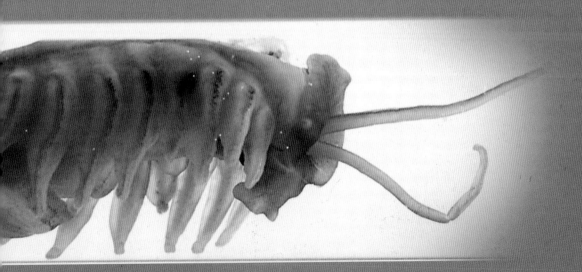

◀ *The parchment worm gives off a gentle glow, particularly from its tail end. The glow may encourage predators to grasp its tail end rather than its head.*

Nasty noises

Some reptiles and amphibians make creepy noises, which can be very loud. Some let out strange screams. Others imitate the noises made by other animals.

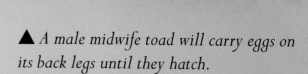
▲ *A male midwife toad will carry eggs on its back legs until they hatch.*

▼ *This smoky frog is swallowing a masked puddle frog whole. As well as other frogs, the smoky frog will eat small birds, mammals and even snakes that are twice its own size.*

Midwife toads

Midwife toads live in northern Africa and parts of Europe. The males make a noise that sounds like an electronic bleep. The females lay strings of eggs, which the males stick to their legs using slime. When the eggs are ready to hatch into tadpoles, the males wade into the water so the tadpoles can swim off.

Smoky frog

The smoky frog, or smoky jungle frog, lives mainly in tropical rainforests in Central and South America. If attacked, the smoky frog makes a high-pitched scream.

▼ *Unlike many frogs, coqui frogs do not have webbed feet. They have discs or pads on their toes that help them to grip onto plants.*

Coqui frogs

The name of these frogs is pronounced co-KEE, which sounds like the noise they make. Coqui frogs originally lived on several Caribbean islands, but they are also found in huge numbers on the islands of Hawaii. They reached Hawaii by accidently hopping aboard cargo ships.

Foul fact!

Coqui frogs make a noise that measures 90 to 100 decibels half a metre from the frog. This is as loud as a speeding express train.

Dirty defences

Birds need to defend themselves from the many predators, including other birds, that hunt them. They have developed many different ways to do this, some of which are quite unpleasant!

▲ *The northern shoveler has a long, spoon-shaped bill for **filter-feeding** from the water. Its webbed feet help it to swim.*

Northern shoveler

The northern shoveler is a **dabbling duck**. It breeds in wetlands across much of North America, northern Europe and Asia. If disturbed by a predator, the female shoveler sprays foul-smelling **faeces** over her eggs to put the predator off eating the eggs.

Petrels

Petrels feed on crabs and fish. Giant petrels also eat **krill**, squid, dead seals and dead penguins. Their stomach contains a thick, strong-smelling oil that they vomit at intruders. The oil makes feathers less waterproof, so it is dangerous for other birds.

◀ *The petrel makes its nest in pebble-lined rock crevices.*

Fulmars

If an intruder approaches a fulmar's nest, the fulmar makes a coughing noise and then spits oil at the attacker. Even fulmar chicks can do this. Very young chicks can spit small amounts of oil as soon as they leave the egg. By the time they are four days old, they can fire oil a distance of 30 centimetres. The chicks may have learned to do this because they are left alone in the nest for long periods while their parents hunt for food at sea.

▼ *The fulmar lays its egg on a grassy cliff edge. Once the chick is about two weeks old, the adult birds leave the nest to search for food.*

▲ *Fulmar chicks use their spitting skills to defend themselves against feral cats, otters, skuas, crows and gulls.*

Disease carriers

Many animals carry diseases that can be passed on to each other, such as **mange** in dogs. Some animals carry diseases that, rather scarily, can be passed on to humans, too.

Dogs and cats

Dogs and cats carry **parasites**, such as **tapeworms** and **roundworms**, which live inside them. The eggs of the parasites pass out in the **faeces** of the dog or cat. People can end up with these parasites, too, if they get the eggs on their hands by touching dogs, and then eat without washing their hands. Regularly '**worming**', or treating, your dog or cat kills the worms.

◀ *It is important to wash your hands after playing with your dog or cat so that you don't pick up any diseases.*

Foul fact!

In the 16th century, pigeon faeces was used to make gunpowder, and was considered to be very valuable!

Pigeons

Many towns around the world have large numbers of pigeons. The birds can carry a disease that affects their lungs and the lungs of people. Symptoms of the disease are mild in pigeons, but can be serious in humans. People catch the disease by breathing in dust containing specks of the birds' faeces. **Bacteria** in the faeces can give a person a fever.

▲ *Be careful not to hold pigeons if you feed them, as this carries a health risk and is not a good idea.*

Rats

Rats live almost everywhere that people live. They spread many diseases, including food poisoning, **typhus** and **bubonic plague**. In the 14th century, the plague became known as the Black Death. It was passed on to humans by infected fleas from the rats. The Black Death may have killed as many as 50 million people in Europe.

▶ *Rats eat the food in our rubbish. Many live near us, in the **sewers** beneath the streets.*

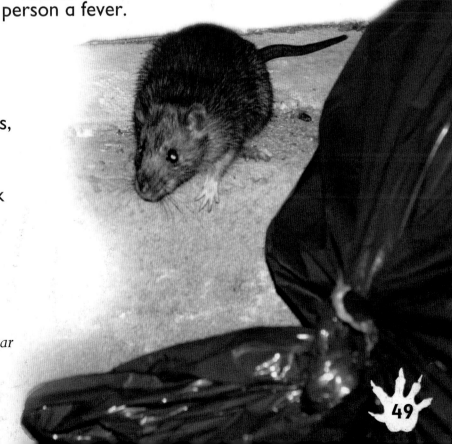

Peculiar predators

Fish have some strange habits when it comes to catching food. Some eat fish bigger than themselves. Others slash at their prey with a sword!

▼ *Oarfish have no teeth. They sieve small creatures through **gill rakers** in their mouths.*

Swordfish

The swordfish is named after its long, sharp bill, which looks like a sword and is at least one-third of the fish's length. The fish can grow up to 4.5 metres long. Feeding mostly at night, it uses its snout to slash at prey. The swordfish rises to the surface looking for fish, such as mackerel, bluefish, silver hake, butterfish and herring, as well as squid.

Oarfish

There are four species of oarfish, or ribbonfish, one of which is the longest **bony fish** in the sea. It can grow to an incredible 15.5 metres long – about the width of a netball court. Oarfish live in the deep ocean and have rarely been seen alive. Occasionally they wash ashore, giving rise to stories about sea serpents.

Black swallower

The black swallower is a light-producing fish that lives up to 1500 metres below the surface in tropical and **subtropical** waters. It has the amazing ability to stretch its stomach up to three times its size when it eats, so that it can eat fish bigger than itself.

▲ *The black swallower opens its mouth wide to eat fish whole and then slowly digests the meal.*

▼ *The swordfish uses its bill to defend itself from predators, such as the shortfin mako shark. Very few predators are fast enough to catch a speeding swordfish.*

Foul fact!

Swordfish have been known to push their swords through the sides of small fishing boats.

Bulgy bodies

Some creepy crawlies have large, bulging bodies. The body of a queen termite is so big she can hardly move.

Hercules moth caterpillar

The caterpillar of the Hercules moth lives in the rainforests of Australia. It is named after the ancient Greek hero Hercules. According to legend, he was the strongest man in the world. The caterpillar turns into one of the world's largest moths. An adult Hercules moth has a wingspan of up to 30 centimetres, making it about the size of a dinner plate.

Termites

Termites have lived on Earth for an amazing 200 million years. There are more than 2500 species. Termites live in **colonies** made up of one or several large, egg-laying queens and thousands, or even millions, of much smaller **worker** and **soldier** termites. The queen termite can lay up to 86,000 eggs in one day.

Foul fact!

The female Hercules moth has no mouth for feeding. All she does before she dies is mate and lay eggs.

◄ *The Hercules moth caterpillar has a large, squishy body covered in yellow spikes. It feeds on the leaves of the bleeding heart tree.*

▲ *After mating, a queen termite loses her wings and she starts a new colony. The head and legs of this queen are visible on the left.*

Termite mounds

Termites build huge nests. Some species build them as tall, clay mounds. Others build them in tree bases and underground. In the forest, termites have a useful job as 'rubbish removers'. They chew up dead wood, making it decay quickly. This makes the soil rich and a good place for plants to grow. In towns, termites can be a pest, as they chew up the wood in houses. In the United States, termites cause more damage to property than storms and fires combined.

▶ *Termite mounds on the African grasslands generally range from about 1 to 3 metres tall. Many of them are about the height of an adult man.*

Weird and wonderful

Some fish look as though they have come straight from the pages of a comic. One looks like a stilt walker, another has a mouth like a cartoon duck, and one is shaped like a guitar!

Foul fact!

The name 'snipe eel' comes from the jaws of the fish, which look like the bill of a wading bird called a snipe.

Tripod fish

The tripod fish lives at the bottom of the **equatorial** oceans. It stands on its three long fins and waits for tiny **crustaceans** to bump into the fins near its head. Then the fish grasps its prey with these fins and directs the prey into its mouth.

◄ The tripod fish only grows up to 37 centimetres long, but its three long fins may extend to nearly one metre long!

Snipe eels

Snipe eels can be as long as 1.5 metres. Their two jaws bend away from each other at the tips, and their teeth hook backwards. This helps them to catch shrimps. Snipe eels prefer to swim in open water rather than near the bottom or the surface.

▲ *Snipe eels swim with their mouths open, and catch the long antennae of passing shrimps on the hooked teeth on their jaws.*

Shovelnose guitarfish

The shovelnose guitarfish was living before the time of dinosaurs. It lives in the **Gulf of California**, and is shaped roughly like a guitar. The shovelnose guitarfish eats crustaceans, such as crabs and shrimps, that it finds on the sea bed. It has lots of small, round teeth that look a little like pebbles.

▶ *The shovelnose guitarfish prefers to live in shallow water. Buried in the sandy sea bed, it can be difficult to spot.*

Nasty noses

Some animals have amazing noses, which they use to seek out food. They may smell their **prey** from a long way off, or use their sensitive noses to detect movements made by their prey.

▲ *The star-nosed mole's tentacles help it to identify prey by touch, as it is blind.*

Star-nosed mole

The star-nosed mole of North America looks like an ordinary mole — except for its nose. 22 fleshy tentacles stick out from the nose and wriggle constantly. They help the mole to feel movements in the ground made by its prey, such as worms.

Aardvark

The aardvark lives in Africa in the area south of the Sahara Desert. It has a long **snout**, which it uses to sniff out its food — ants and termites — as it walks along at night. It may walk as far as 30 kilometres in one night, pressing its nose to the ground to pick up their scent. It also listens for any sound of movement made by the termites.

▶ *When an aardvark digs a burrow or breaks into a termite mound, it can squeeze its nostrils shut to keep out the dust.*

▶ *The nose of the male proboscis monkey can be up to 14 centimetres long. It makes the monkey's warning calls louder.*

Foul fact!

A male proboscis monkey pushes its nose out of the way when it eats!

Proboscis monkey

The proboscis monkey is named after the large, wobbly nose, or 'proboscis', of the male monkey. It is thought that the large nose helps the male to attract a mate. It lives in the swampy mangrove forests of Borneo, and wades through the water on its back legs. This makes it very unusual, as most monkeys move around using all four legs.

Bully boys

Birds can be vicious, both to other birds and to humans. Some birds attack other birds to kill and eat them. Some fight other birds to steal the food they have caught. Some attack to protect their chicks.

Great skua

The great skua is an aggressive bird with a wingspan of about 1.4 metres. Some people call it the pirate of the seas. It attacks other birds and steals their prey, and kills and eats puffins and kittiwakes. Skuas also eat fish, **lemmings** and the eggs and young of other birds.

Magpies

Magpies are common birds often seen in the United Kingdom and Australia. They attack and eat the eggs and young of other birds, including chickens, and are often shot as **vermin** by farmers. The Australian magpie is a particularly aggressive species. A survey found that nine out of ten Australian men had been attacked by a magpie at some time in their lives!

◀ *Male Australian magpies often attack people on bikes, who they may see as being a threat to their newly hatched chicks.*

▼ *The great skua makes harsh screams or barks when attacking intruders.*

Cuckoos

Many types of cuckoo have a bullying habit. The common cuckoo, for example, lays an egg in the nest of a smaller bird. The cuckoo's egg hatches first, and the small bird feeds the young cuckoo, which grows quickly. The cuckoo soon pushes the eggs or chicks of the smaller bird out of the nest.

▶ *The young cuckoo is much bigger than the adult foster bird.*

Slippery at sea

The sea has a huge variety of slimy, slippery beasts hidden in its depths. One of them, the giant squid, is as large as a sailing yacht. You wouldn't want to get wrapped up in its long, slimy **tentacles**!

◀ *Not many creatures are big enough to hunt the giant squid, but sperm whales and sleeper sharks will attack them.*

Giant squid

Giant squid live in deep water in all of the world's oceans, but they are rare in tropical and polar areas. They grow to huge sizes. Females can be up to 13 metres long and males up to 10 metres long, making them one of the biggest slimy creatures alive.

▼ *The sea hare's skin contains a slimy poison that makes it a nasty meal for predators.*

Sea hares

Sea hares are large, slimy sea slugs. They only eat plants that are the same colour as themselves. Sea hares use their colour for camouflage, hiding in seaweed. When scared, a sea hare squirts out ink to confuse predators, such as sea anemones.

Starfish

Starfish are found in all of the Earth's oceans. Scientists have been collecting starfish slime because they have found that it contains a material that may be useful in treating **allergies**, such as hay fever.

▼ *Many starfish eat clams and oysters. To get at the creature inside the shell, the starfish has to prise the two parts of the shell apart using the suckers on its arms.*

Foul fact!

A starfish has two stomachs. To help it digest food, it can push one stomach out through its mouth.

Poisonous pests

Some reptiles and amphibians are very poisonous. They might have poison in their skin, their **saliva** or their **venomous** fangs.

▼ *The horned viper has two long scales on its head that look like horns. The horns may help to protect the snake's eyes, and may also make the snake harder for predators to spot.*

Horned viper

The horned viper lives in northern Africa and parts of the Middle East. When hunting, it digs its body into the sand and lies in wait. The only parts of the snake that remain visible are its horns. When prey approaches it suddenly lurches out of the sand and strikes, shooting poison from its fangs. The horned viper preys on unwary **rodents**, such as rats, as well as small snakes, lizards and birds.

A drug made from the saliva of the Gila monster is being used in the United States to treat diabetes.

▲ *The Gila monster has powerful claws for digging burrows but kills with poisonous saliva.*

Gila monster

The Gila monster is a lizard. It kills and eats birds, rodents and other lizards by biting them and then chewing until venomous saliva flows into the wound. The Gila monster lives in the south-west of the United States and in northern Mexico. Its teeth are loose and if a few get broken, it just grows some more.

Poison-dart frogs

Poison-dart frogs are found in Central and South America and most are brightly coloured to warn predators that they are dangerous to eat. They **secrete**, or release, poison through their skin.

▶ *The most toxic poison-dart frog is the golden poison frog, which carries enough poison to kill up to ten humans.*

Scavengers

Lots of birds find their food by scavenging. They may eat parts of carcasses left behind by other animals, or they may scavenge for food on rubbish dumps. Whichever they choose, it can be a messy business.

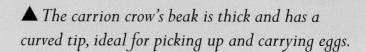

▲ *The carrion crow's beak is thick and has a curved tip, ideal for picking up and carrying eggs.*

Carrion crow

The carrion crow is a large, black bird that likes to sit on the top of isolated trees so it can spy on the surrounding countryside. It watches birds building their nests, and later attacks them, eating their eggs and young.

Crested caracara

The crested caracara, or Mexican eagle, is the national bird of Mexico. It prefers to eat carrion in the form of dead and rotting fish, or roadkill. Sometimes it will attack brown pelicans and force them to **disgorge** the fish they have caught.

◄ *The male caracara often acts as a lookout, watching for danger from a perch near its nest, to protect its young.*

Marabou stork

The marabou stork is a large bird. Its wingspan can reach a huge 3.2 metres – the largest wingspan of any land bird, matched only by the Andean condor. The marabou stork scavenges on carrion and scraps. This may sound unpleasant, but it helps prevent the spread of diseases.

Foul fact!

Marabou storks march in front of grass fires, snatching and eating the small animals that are fleeing.

▶ *The marabou stork's featherless head and neck are easy to keep clean as it feeds.*

Fish in the freezer

Even in very cold water, fish can survive. The freezing waters of the Southern Ocean are home to at least 270 species of fish. The fish that live there need to be specially adapted so they do not freeze solid in the extremely cold temperatures.

Blackfin icefish

The blackfin icefish has a type of natural **antifreeze** in its blood that prevents ice crystals forming in its body. This helps it to survive in sub-zero temperatures. It has no red blood cells, so its blood carries less oxygen than most fish. To make up for this, it has a large heart that beats twice as fast as other fish. It lives in the Southern Ocean and southern Atlantic Ocean.

▼ *The blackfin icefish spends most of its time resting at the bottom of the sea. They do not move very much due to the cold.*

Snailfish

Snailfish live in both cold and warm waters, at shallow depths and as deep as 7500 metres. One-third of their body weight is a jelly-like substance made mostly of water. This makes the fish more buoyant, or able to keep afloat.

▲ *Snailfish have pink and grey, jelly-like bodies. They look like giant tadpoles in shape.*

Foul fact!

Some Antarctic fish can die of heatstroke if the temperature rises above a chilly 6 degrees Celsius.

Bald notothen

The bald notothen is another fish that has a special **protein** in its blood that stops it freezing in the cold waters of the Antarctic. This fish lives underneath the ice shelf, where it eats tiny krill and larvae.

▲ *To keep themselves safe from predators, newly hatched bald notothen swim up into the ice that lies several metres below the surface.*

Sneaky salamanders

Many salamander species are known for having a sneaky trick. If a predator grabs the salamander by the tail, part of the tail breaks off and wriggles about like a separate creature. This distracts the predator so the salamander can run away unharmed.

▼ *Mole salamanders have smooth, shiny skin that can absorb oxygen.*

Fire salamander

The fire salamander lives in the forests of southern and central Europe. It hunts mainly at dusk and during the night for insects, spiders, slugs, worms and other small creatures, such as newts and young frogs. When it is not hunting, it hides under stones and logs.

Mole salamanders

Mole salamanders live in North America, in woodland and grassland areas. They live in burrows that they have dug, or in holes abandoned by other small creatures. Some mole salamanders spend all winter in their burrows, but return to the ponds where they were born when it is time to breed.

▼ *If threatened, the fire salamander sprays a poisonous, milky fluid from glands along its back at the predator.*

Hellbenders

Hellbenders, or giant salamanders, live in Japan, China and North America. The two North American species grow up to 40 centimetres long, but their Japanese cousin grows up to 1.8 metres long. Hellbenders eat virtually any living thing that they find in the water, including **crayfish**, worms and insects.

Foul fact!

In North America, hellbenders have many names including devil dog and snot otter!

▶ *Hellbenders have wrinkly skin that oozes slime. The slime protects them from cuts and attacks from parasites.*

Squishy sea life

Some sea creatures have very soft bodies. Animals that are too squishy to live on land can survive in the ocean because they are supported by the water.

▲ *A sea cucumber has hundreds of sticky suction-cup feet that it uses to crawl around on the sea bed.*

▼ *The sea anemone's tentacles enable it to catch prey, such as small fish.*

Sea cucumbers

Sea cucumbers have warty skin and soft spines. When they are scared, they squeeze their muscles and shoot water out of their bodies. Some sea cucumbers even shoot out their **intestines** at predators to scare them off. Then they grow new intestines.

Sea anemones

Jelly-like sea anemones can be as small as 1.25 centimetres, and some as huge as 1.8 metres. Their mouth is in the centre, surrounded by a ring of tentacles. These tentacles feel sticky to touch, and are used to catch and kill prey. At the slightest touch, the tentacles fire a tiny spike into the prey, injecting it with paralyzing poison.

Box jellyfish

Box jellyfish are sometimes called sea wasps. They look like nearly transparent, box-shaped jellyfish, but they are not actually jellyfish at all. One highly **venomous** species is about the size of a basketball. It has long tentacles that drift behind it as it swims. The tentacles are covered in stinging cells that it uses to kill prey, such as shrimp and small fish.

▼ Box jellyfish have been called the deadliest creature in the animal kingdom. It is thought they may have killed more than 5500 people since 1954.

Foul fact!

The venom from some box jellyfish can kill a human in less than 4 minutes!

Loathsome legs

Spiders are not the only creepy crawlies with scary legs. The massive Japanese spider crab has ten legs, at least as long as a tall man!

Japanese spider crab

The Japanese spider crab lives in the Pacific Ocean around Japan. Using its two front legs, which are specialized for feeding, it eats mainly dead animals and shellfish that it finds on the seabed. It is preyed on by even bigger octopuses and by fishermen.

▲ *Scolopendra centipedes grasp their prey with the claws on the ends of their powerful legs.*

Scolopendra centipedes

Scolopendra centipedes can be more than 30 centimetres long – longer than a school ruler. Most scolopendra centipedes are **nocturnal**. They hunt at night for insects and mice.

Using a pair of poison claws directly under the head, they bite their prey again and again, injecting it with venom. The bite of a scolopendra centipede can be very painful to a human.

◀ *The Japanese spider crab has a legspan about as long as a small car.*

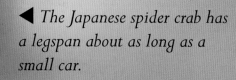

▼ *The basic structure of a harvestman has not changed much in 400 million years.*

Harvestmen

Harvestmen belong to a big family – there are more than 6400 species worldwide. They eat flies, mites, small slugs, spiders, decaying plants, **fungi** and bird droppings. After each meal, the harvestman pulls each of its eight legs through its jaws, one at a time, to clean them. If a harvestman is attacked by a bird, it releases a terrible stink as a defense.

Foul fact!
If a harvestman is attacked and loses a leg, the leg continues to twitch. The predator is distracted and the harvestman escapes.

Poisonous animals

There are many types of poisonous creature around the world. Some animals use **venom** for defence. Others use it to catch larger prey.

▲ *The duck-billed platypus has a flat bill like a duck's beak, a furry body and strong limbs that help it to swim and dig.*

Duck-billed platypus

The duck-billed platypus lives in eastern Australia. It eats frogs, fish and insects. The male platypus has a **spur** on each of its back legs, which holds a strong poison. If threatened, the platypus stabs its attacker with a spur and injects the poison. The poison is strong enough to kill a dog.

Solenodons

The two species of solenodon are both **endangered**. They live on the Caribbean islands of Hispaniola and Cuba. When a solenodon attacks its prey, such as a spider, poisonous **saliva** flows into its victim along grooves in its lower front teeth. The poison stuns the prey, making it easier to grasp.

◀ *Solenodons run on their toes, and often trip over if they try to run too fast.*

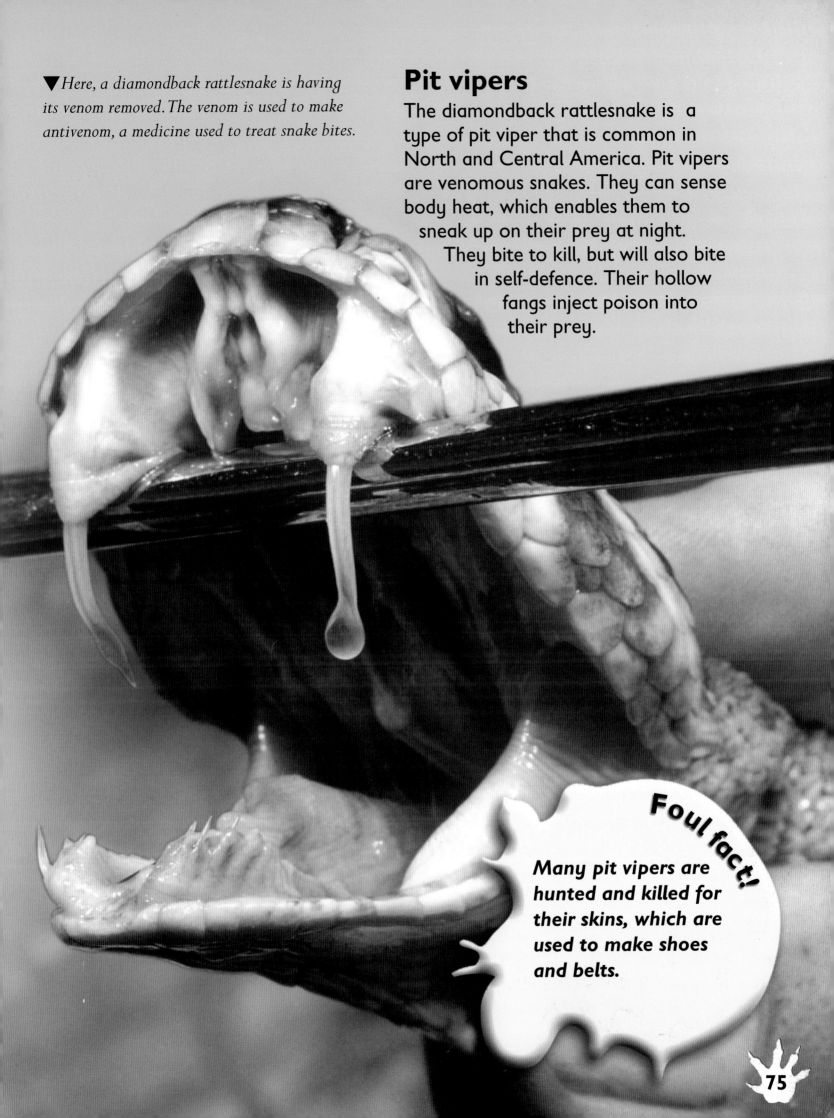

▼ *Here, a diamondback rattlesnake is having its venom removed. The venom is used to make antivenom, a medicine used to treat snake bites.*

Pit vipers

The diamondback rattlesnake is a type of pit viper that is common in North and Central America. Pit vipers are venomous snakes. They can sense body heat, which enables them to sneak up on their prey at night. They bite to kill, but will also bite in self-defence. Their hollow fangs inject poison into their prey.

Foul fact!

Many pit vipers are hunted and killed for their skins, which are used to make shoes and belts.

Vicious animals

Animals, such as killer whales, tigers and bears, are well known for being fierce. However, the world is also full of small, vicious creatures that hunt their prey aggressively.

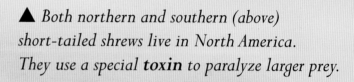

▲ *Both northern and southern (above) short-tailed shrews live in North America. They use a special* **toxin** *to paralyze larger prey.*

Northern short-tailed shrew

The northern short-tailed shrew is small, but very fierce! It needs to eat three times its body weight each day, so it spends its time hunting for insects, spiders, worms and snails.

▶ *Weasels prey on mice, voles, frogs, birds and rabbits. They eat eggs, too!*

Weasels

Weasels live mainly in the **northern hemisphere**. The weasel is a savage hunter. Its long, slender body allows it to follow its prey into small burrows. When excited, weasels do a strange, hopping war dance. Some **biologists** believe they perform the dance to confuse their prey.

Foul fact!

Various words are used to describe a group of weasels including a gang, pack, confusion and boogle!

Tasmanian devil

The Tasmanian devil looks like a small bear and is very vicious. It uses its powerful jaws to crack bones and tear fur and flesh, before eating the lot. As well as feeding on carrion – animals that are already dead – it also eats the **larvae** of some types of beetle, and attacks poultry.

▼ *The Tasmanian devil was named 'devil' because of the high-pitched screeching noises it makes at night. When threatened, it opens its mouth in a yawn, which looks aggressive but is a display of fear.*

Slimy pond life

Ponds are seething with slimy life. Hiding behind rocks, slipping through the water and slithering through the weeds are slimy creatures of all shapes and sizes.

▲ *A medicinal leech has three jaws that move backwards and forwards as the leech drinks blood.*

Medicinal leech

Doctors used to think that when people were ill, they would benefit from having some of their blood drained off. To remove the blood, the doctors used leeches. The medicinal leech uses **suction** and slime to attach itself to its prey, or to a person. As it sucks the blood of its prey, the leech dribbles saliva into the wound, making the blood easier to drink.

Foul fact!

The body of a medicinal leech stretches to about 10 times its original size as it fills with blood.

Newts

Newts are found in North America, Europe and Asia. They spend part of their time on land, but they start their lives in fresh water. Newts lay a single egg on plants in ponds or slow-moving streams. They often wrap the egg in a leaf to protect it. The egg hatches into a **larva** with feathery **gills**. Gradually the gills get smaller and the larva grows legs. The young newt, called an eft, is then able to leave the water.

▼ *The poisonous slime of the rough-skinned newt will kill most predators except the common gartersnake, which is **immune** to the poison.*

▲ *Sludge worms live with their heads stuck in the mud and their tails waving in the water.*

Sludge worm

The sludge worm lives in large colonies on the bottom of ponds. It can survive even in very polluted water. The worm eats tiny pieces of food found in the mud that it slurps up.

Nasty nippers

Some creepy crawlers have pincers at their tail end. In some species these are harmless, but in others they can give a nasty nip.

Hellgrammites

Hellgrammites are the larvae of dobsonflies. They hide under rocks in fast-flowing streams and wait for prey to pass. Then they pounce. When the larvae are 2 to 3 years old, they crawl out of the water and burrow into damp soil. Two weeks later, they emerge as adult dobsonflies, and only live for about two more weeks.

Earwigs

There are about 1800 species of earwigs, and at least one of them probably lives in your garden. Earwigs are mainly nocturnal. During the day, they hide in dark cracks and under stones. At night, they hunt for other insects, plants and ripe fruit. Some earwigs use their nippers to hold on to prey or to grip their mate when mating.

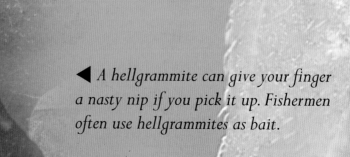

◄ *A hellgrammite can give your finger a nasty nip if you pick it up. Fishermen often use hellgrammites as bait.*

Foul fact!
Long ago, people believed that earwigs crawled inside the ears of people as they slept and burrowed into their brains.

▲ *Many species of earwig have nippers that look fearsome, but are actually soft and cannot hurt humans. Earwigs can open and close their nippers like scissors.*

Diplurans

Diplurans look like tiny, pale earwigs. They have pincers at their tail end. To catch prey, a dipluran burrows into soft soil until only its pincers are above ground. If tiny creatures, such as springtails or insect larvae, pass by, the dipluran snatches them into its burrow and eats them. Some species eat only rotting plant material.

▶ *Diplurans do not have eyes. Instead they have light detectors to help them find their way about.*

81

Vicious vampires

▼ The candirú's body is almost see-through, making it hard to spot as it swims in the River Amazon.

Vampires are not only found in creepy castles at Hallowe'en! Some fish also suck blood from living creatures, and others have extremely scary teeth.

Candirú

The candirú is a tiny freshwater fish that lives in the River Amazon. To find its prey, it tastes the water to detect a water stream coming from the **gills** of another fish. It follows the stream and slips inside the fish's gills. Spines around the candirú's head dig into the prey fish and hold the candirú in place so that it can feed on the fish's blood.

▼ A viperfish is seen here chasing a small prey fish. Viperfish hunt at night in fairly shallow water, luring prey with their photophores. They return to much deeper water by day.

Viperfish

Viperfish are among the fiercest predators of the deep. A viperfish's sharp, fanglike teeth are so long that they do not fit inside its mouth, but curve back close to the fish's eyes. The viperfish uses its teeth to stab its victims. It swims at them at speed and spikes them.

Common fangtooth

The common fangtooth is a really scary-looking, deep-sea fish. It gets its name from the sharp fangs that stick out of its enormous mouth. Despite its fearsome appearance, it mainly eats tiny **zooplankton**, as well as any other creatures that float or get sucked into its gaping mouth.

▶ *When the common fangtooth shuts its mouth, the two long teeth on the bottom jaw slip into two tubes on either side of the fish's brain.*

Foul fact!

The common fangtooth is so ugly that its nickname is 'ogrefish'!

Beware dragons!

Some reptiles look like dragons and are even called dragons. They have scaly skin, long claws and some have spikes all down their back.

▲ Like many lizards, the Chinese water dragon can sense light through a small bump on the top of its head called a '**third eye**'.

Komodo dragon

The Komodo dragon of Indonesia grows up to 3 metres long and is the largest species of lizard. It has a big appetite and can eat up to 80 percent of its body weight in one meal. It eats other reptiles, birds, monkeys, goats, deer, horses and water buffaloes.

Chinese water dragon

The Chinese water dragon lives in the rainforests of South East Asia. It often sits on branches overhanging water, and if startled, drops into the water and swims away. It can stay underwater for up to 30 minutes. The Chinese water dragon eats insects, small fish, rodents and plants.

◀ The Komodo dragon has long claws for catching hold of prey. It bites off chunks of meat with its teeth. Its saliva is filled with bacteria that help to kill its prey quickly.

Green iguana

The green iguana looks like a wingless dragon. It grows up to 2 metres long and has pointed scales along its back. Although it looks fierce, the green iguana is a herbivore, which means it eats only plants. It lives in Central and South America.

▲ *The green iguana's long fingers and claws enable it to climb trees and cling onto branches.*

Bizarre birds

Some birds look as if they have been put together using the different parts of other birds! From birds with strange beaks to birds with peculiar habits, there are some very Bizarre birds in the world.

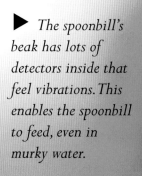

▶ The spoonbill's beak has lots of detectors inside that feel vibrations. This enables the spoonbill to feed, even in murky water.

Secretary bird

The secretary bird lives in Africa. It appears on the coat of arms, or state emblem, of Sudan and South Africa. The bird has an unusual habit — it stamps hard on grassy **tussocks** with its feet. This scares any small lizards, **mammals**, birds or grasshoppers that may be hiding there. As they run away, the secretary bird stamps on them to stun or squash them. Then it tears them apart using its hooked beak.

◀ The secretary bird has long, skinny legs like a **wading bird**, and a body like an eagle.

Sun bittern

The sun bittern is found in Central and South America. The adult birds perform a special 'broken wing' trick to protect their nest. If a predator approaches, the sun bittern will drag one wing along the ground as if it is broken. The predator will follow the apparently injured bird, thinking it will be easy to catch.

▶ *When the sun bittern is scared, it raises its wings to show off two large eye spots. The 'eyes' make the bird's body look like the head of a much bigger, scarier animal.*

Foul fact!

Spoonbill chicks sometimes die from starvation while their parents take too long looking for food.

Spoonbills

Spoonbills wade through shallow water, swinging their open bill from side to side in the water. If any small fish, insects or **crustaceans** touch the inside of the bill, the bird snaps it shut!

Hard to spot

Fish have some very clever disguises. They can be so well camouflaged that they are virtually impossible to spot. Some look like lumps of stone, others look like pieces of seaweed.

▼ *The devil scorpionfish looks as if it has weed or **algae** growing on it. Its skin changes colour slightly to blend with its surroundings.*

▲ *The bristle-bushmouth catfish's wormlike bristles draw prey close to the fish.*

Bristle-bushmouth catfish

The bristle-bushmouth catfish lives in the rivers of South America. It has long, bristly tentacles on its snout that it uses to find food. This has led to it being called the Medusa Head. In Greek mythology, Medusa was a monstrous woman who had snakes for hair. She could turn people into stone.

Devil scorpionfish

The devil scorpionfish is a master of disguise. It looks like a rock or chunk of dead coral. The fish has **venomous** spines on its back and fins that it can raise to defend itself. The poison can be fatal to humans.

Leafy sea dragon

The leafy sea dragon is a close relative of sea horses. It lives in the warm oceans around Australia. As with sea horses, the females lay the eggs, but the males carry them in a pouch until they hatch.

▶ *The leafy shapes on the sea dragon help it to hide among floating seaweed or **kelp** beds.*

Sneaky animals

Some animals use sneaky methods to catch their prey or to escape from predators. They may use disguises, move quietly or use clever tricks.

▲ *The vampire bat quietly creeps along the ground up to its prey, such as a cow or a pig.*

Vampire bats

Vampire bats are found in Africa and South America. The common vampire bat is able to walk, jump and hop. This means it can creep up to its prey and hop onto its body. As it bites, the bat's saliva enters the wound and makes the animal's skin go numb. The animal does not know it has been bitten.

Tarsiers

Tarsiers are related to monkeys and lemurs. They are found on islands in South East Asia. Tarsiers have good eyesight and hunt mostly at night, jumping onto their prey, which includes insects, birds and snakes. They pounce and grab the animal with their paws.

◀ *Tarsiers have large pads at the end of long fingers, to help grip branches and prey tightly.*

Many people think of raccoons as pests because the animals spill the rubbish from bins in streets and gardens.

Raccoons

Raccoons are very sneaky. Their specially adapted paws can open latches and doors. Their black eye patches make them look like masked bandits – and they can act like them, too! They often steal food from houses, cars and campsites.

▲ *Raccoons often rifle through rubbish bins in search of food.*

Big mouth

Some birds, such as pelicans, have a huge mouth that they use to snap up large prey. Other birds use their mouth to alarm predators. The bird may suddenly open its mouth wide to startle its enemy.

▲ *If frightened, a tawny frogmouth opens its beak wide and shows its yellow throat, hoping to scare away predators.*

Tawny frogmouth

The tawny frogmouth lives in Australia. By day, it sits very still in trees and is difficult to spot. At night, it hunts for insects, which it may dig from the soil or catch while flying. The tawny frogmouth either beats its prey to death or swallows it whole.

Toucans

Toucans live in the rainforests of South America. They use their huge, colourful bills to pick fruit to eat. The length of the bill enables them to reach fruit on branches that are too small to take their weight. During the mating season, male and female toucans throw fruit at each other to attract a mate.

◄ *The toucan's large bill may put off predators, but it is not strong enough to be used as a weapon.*

Pelicans

Pelicans are water birds found on many of the world's coastlines. A large pouch hangs under their beak. They eat fish, frogs and crustaceans, such as crabs and shrimps. Sometimes they also eat smaller birds.

▼ *Pelicans expand their throat pouch to scoop prey out of the water. They drain off the water before swallowing the prey.*

Foul fact!

In medieval times, it was thought that mother pelicans fed their young with their own blood when food was scarce.

Bizarre creatures

Reptiles and amphibians have some amazing habits. One lizard, the common basilisk, can actually run across water.

Common basilisk

A young common basilisk can run about 10 to 20 metres across the surface of water without sinking. It does this when fleeing from predators. The common basilisk lives near streams and lakes in the rainforests of Central and South America. It eats insects, flowers and small creatures, such as fish, snakes and birds.

▶ *Webbing between the toes of the common basilisk helps it to run across water. On land, the webbing is rolled up.*

▲ *Common rain frogs get their name from their habit of calling during rainstorms.*

Common rain frogs

Tiny common rain frogs live in the rainforests of Central and South America, on some Caribbean islands and in southern Africa. They lay their eggs in a cup of leaves or on a moist patch of the forest floor. The eggs hatch into frogs rather than tadpoles.

Foul fact!
According to legend, the basilisk could kill things just by looking at them.

Jackson's chameleon

The Jackson's chameleon comes from eastern Africa and has been introduced in Hawaii. The babies are born fully developed, rather than hatching from eggs.

◀ *The Jackson's chameleon is able to look in two directions at once. Males have three long horns.*

Beastly beetles

The Ancient Egyptians believed that scarabs, or dung beetles, kept the world revolving like a huge ball of dung, or **faeces**. They worshipped the beetles and carved huge statues of them in some of their temples.

Dung beetles

Dung beetles live in many different **habitats**, including deserts, forests and grasslands. They feed on the animal dung of plant-eating animals, such as rabbits, cattle and elephants. Dung beetles squeeze and suck liquid out of the manure.

▼ *Using their back legs, some dung beetles roll animal dung into balls larger than themselves, and use these balls as a supply of food.*

Burying beetles

Burying beetles bury dead creatures, such as birds or mice, in a hole in the soil. They strip the feathers or fur from the dead creature and line the hole with the material. The female lays her eggs in the soil around the hole. When the eggs hatch, the larvae move into the dead body to feed.

◀ *Burying beetles use their antennae to detect dead animals, such as this slug, from a long way off.*

Foul fact!

Some burying beetles regurgitate the flesh of dead creatures to feed their young.

Stag beetles

Stag beetle larvae live for several years, eating rotting wood. They can be found in the woodlands of southern and central Europe, and also in parks and gardens that have tree stumps or logs. The larvae change, or **metamorphose**, into beetles. In summer, the beetles fly about, rather clumsily, in search of mates.

▶ *Male stag beetles have enormous jaws that resemble a stag's antlers. They use them to fight rival males for the best mating sites.*

Soil sliders

Foul fact!

A flatworm gets rid of its faeces through the same opening that it uses to take in food.

Slimy creatures lurk in the soil and on plant leaves. Some use their slimy **faeces** as a disguise, some produce poisonous slime to ward off predators, and some simply use slime to slither along.

▼ *Covered in their own faeces, lily beetle larvae eat up lily leaves, starting at the tips and working their way back to the stem.*

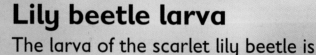

Lily beetle larva

The larva of the scarlet lily beetle is very slimy. It hatches from its egg and covers itself in its own wet, slimy faeces, so that it looks a bit like a bird dropping. This helps to keep it safe from predators. Scarlet lily beetles are serious pests that eat the leaves of lilies and other plants, causing lots of damage.

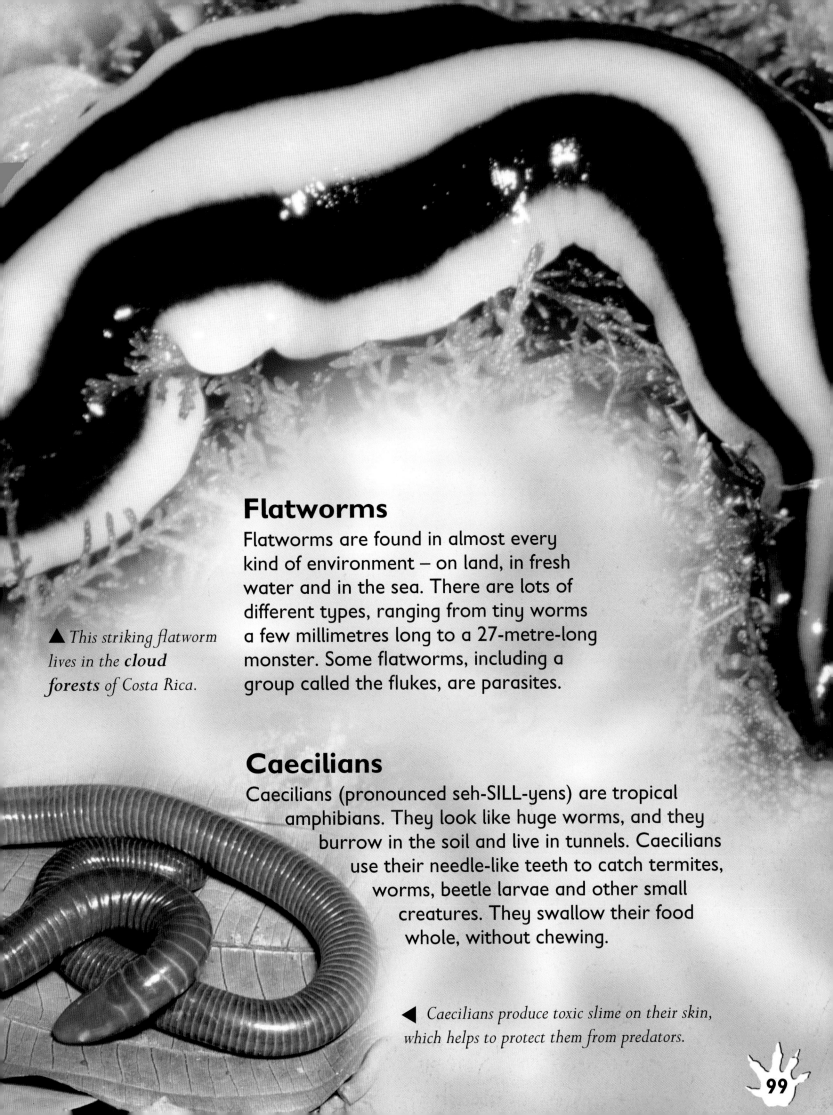

Flatworms

Flatworms are found in almost every kind of environment – on land, in fresh water and in the sea. There are lots of different types, ranging from tiny worms a few millimetres long to a 27-metre-long monster. Some flatworms, including a group called the flukes, are parasites.

▲ *This striking flatworm lives in the **cloud forests** of Costa Rica.*

Caecilians

Caecilians (pronounced seh-SILL-yens) are tropical amphibians. They look like huge worms, and they burrow in the soil and live in tunnels. Caecilians use their needle-like teeth to catch termites, worms, beetle larvae and other small creatures. They swallow their food whole, without chewing.

◀ *Caecilians produce toxic slime on their skin, which helps to protect them from predators.*

Peculiar predators

Some reptiles and amphibians use a **lure** to attract prey. Others wait silently in hiding until prey passes and then launch a sudden attack.

Alligator snapping turtle

The alligator snapping turtle lives in North America. It has a small, wormlike growth on its tongue that it wriggles to attract prey, especially fish. It also eats frogs, small snakes, birds and small animals.

▲ *The death adder has a thick body and a short tail. It takes 2 to 3 years to reach adult size.*

Death adders

Death adders live in Australia and New Guinea. They bury themselves in sand or **leaf litter**, so that only the head and tail are visible. To attract prey, the death adder dangles the tip of its tail, which looks like a worm. When a bird or mammal tries to grab the 'worm', the death adder strikes and poisons its prey in a fraction of a second.

◄ *The alligator snapping turtle's jaws are strong enough to bite off a human finger.*

Surinam horned frog

The Surinam horned frog lives in northern South America. It burrows itself into the ground and waits for prey. If a mouse, small lizard or frog wanders past, the Surinam horned frog jumps out and grabs it.

▼ *The Surinam horned frog is well camouflaged. The pattern on its skin makes it looks like a leaf, so that it is difficult to see on the forest floor.*

Horrid guests

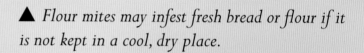

Creepy crawlers are at their creepiest when they share our houses. They appear to watch us from cracks in the wall, or scuttle out from under furniture and make us jump.

▲ Flour mites may infest fresh bread or flour if it is not kept in a cool, dry place.

Flour mites

Flour mites are tiny creatures that live in and feed off flour, grains and seeds. A female flour mite can lay 500 to 800 eggs in her lifetime. Flour infested with mites smells sweet and sickly. If you want to test whether there are mites in your flour, sprinkle some on a flat surface and look at it through a magnifying glass. The flour will become bumpy and uneven, and a tiny creature may emerge.

Silverfish

The silverfish has existed for over 300 million years. It eats the **starch** and sugars found in glue, book bindings, textiles and even the dandruff that falls from our heads. However, it can survive for a year without eating.

◄ The silverfish prefers to live in warm, damp places, such as bathrooms or underneath floors. It can run extremely fast.

Cockroaches

About 25 to 30 cockroach species are regarded as pests. They can carry serious diseases, including **dysentery** and **typhoid**. Cockroaches live all around the world. Some species prefer kitchens and laundries, which get hot and steamy, while others live in forests. They live in groups, hiding by day in dark corners and coming out at night. Some species feed on people's leftover food and rubbish.

▶ *There may be as many as 7500 species of cockroaches. Some types of cockroach can survive for a month without food, and can last without air for 45 minutes.*

Foul fact!

A cockroach's faeces contain chemicals that other cockroaches sniff to find food and water.

Slimy amphibians

Amphibians spend some of the time on land and some of the time in water. They are able to breathe through their skin, which they need to keep damp and slimy.

▲ *The olm is also called the humanfish because its skin is thought to resemble human skin.*

Slimy salamanders

Slimy salamanders live in woodland in the United States. They do not have lungs, but take in air through their skin and the lining of their mouth. Slimy salamanders get their name from the slime that oozes from their skin. If you get it on your hands, it will stick like glue.

▼ *The sticky slime that slimy salamanders produce makes them a nasty meal for predators.*

Olm

The olm lives in caves in parts of Europe. It is albino, which means it has no colour at all in its skin. It is also blind, but has good hearing and a strong sense of smell. The olm preys on crabs, snails and bugs.

Grey foam-nest treefrog

The grey foam-nest treefrog lives mainly in south-east and south-central Africa. It lives in **subtropical** or tropical forests, grassland, shrubland, marshes and even gardens. Foam-nest treefrogs save water in their bodies so that they can live in very dry places. They also produce slime that turns into a waterproof cocoon.

▼ *Pairs of grey foam-nest treefrogs make their foam nest on a branch overhanging rainwater pools. Tadpoles emerge from the eggs, and after about a week drop from the foam into the water below.*

Foul fact!

The grey foam-nest treefrog turns almost white in hot weather. White reflects sunlight, so this helps keep the frog cool.

Peculiar predators

Some birds have horrid hunting habits. They may beat or peck their prey to death, or even push it onto branches or rocks. One bird even drinks the blood of other birds.

▶ *Kookaburras have a loud call that sounds like hysterical laughter.*

Kookaburras

Kookaburras live in Australia, New Zealand and New Guinea. They mainly eat insects, worms and crustaceans, but sometimes vary their diet with small snakes, mammals, frogs and birds. They pounce on their prey from a perch, bashing large victims against a branch or the ground.

Vampire finch

The vampire finch lives on Wolf Island in the **Galápagos**. It feeds on blood, which it gets by pecking at the feet and wings of other birds. It also eats the eggs of seabirds called boobies.

◀ *A vampire finch feeds on the blood of a larger bird.*

European bee-eater

The European bee-eater is a **migratory** bird. It spends winter in warm places such as Africa, north-west India and Sri Lanka, and the summer in Europe. It eats bees, wasps and hornets. Before eating, the bee-eater hits the insect against its perch to knock off the sting. In just one day, the European bee-eater eats as many as 250 bees.

◀ *European bee-eaters build burrow-like nests up to 1.5 metres long in banks or cliffs.*

Poisonous parts

Many fish and other water creatures are poisonous. Most of them only use their poison in self-defence and not for attack.

Weevers

Weevers have poisonous spines on their gills and on their first dorsal fin (dorsal fins are on a fish's back). During the day, weevers bury themselves in the sand on the sea bed, leaving just their eyes poking out. As shrimps and small fish swim past, the weevers snap them up.

 *The blue-ringed octopus is only the size of a golf ball, but it is one of the world's most poisonous animals.*

Blue-ringed octopuses

The blue-ringed octopus is a mollusc, not a fish. Blue-ringed octopuses live in tide pools in the Pacific Ocean, from Australia to Japan. A blue-ringed octopus will camouflage itself as it hunts for crabs and shrimps. If attacked by a predator, it turns bright yellow with blue rings, and bites the attacker. Its poison is created by bacteria in the octopus's **salivary glands**. A single octopus carries enough poison to kill 26 adults.

◀ *The weever's poison is for defence. If a person stood on the fish, the fish's spines would sink into their foot. This would release a poison that causes a great deal of pain — worse than a wasp sting.*

▼ *The stonefish is the most venomous fish in the world. It can be very difficult to spot among the reef's rocks.*

Stonefish

The stonefish lives on coral reefs in the shallow, tropical waters of the Indian and Pacific oceans. Its mottled colours provide good camouflage among the rocks. The stonefish eats shrimps, small fish and crustaceans. The dorsal fin on its back is covered in many venomous spines. The poison can be fatal to humans.

Foul fact!

Poison from the stonefish causes very severe pain to people who touch them.

Terrifying tongues

Some animals have an amazing tongue. It may be forked, sticky or just incredibly long. Tongues can be used for digging insects from the ground or grabbing leaves and branches.

▲ *An echidna hunts by poking its nose into the ground, leaving behind cone-shaped nose prints.*

Echidnas

Echidnas, or spiny anteaters, live in Australia, Tasmania and New Guinea. They have small nostrils and a tiny mouth at the end of their long, tubelike beaks. They eat ants and termites, which they catch with their long, sticky tongue.

Okapi

The okapi is brown with a stripy **rump** and legs. It is related to the giraffe. A shy animal, it lives in the dense forests of the African Congo and was only discovered in 1901. The okapi uses its long, black tongue to grab leaves and branches and pull them into its mouth.

◀ *The okapi's tongue is is 35 centimetres long. It is as sensitive and flexible as a human hand.*

Sun bear

The sun bear lives in the forests of South East Asia. It likes to make its home high up in the branches of trees. The sun bear sleeps or sunbathes by day and hunts at night. It has long, curved claws, which it uses to dig for insects. It also pokes its long tongue into holes in rotten wood to catch insects or lick up honey.

▶ *The sun bear's slithery tongue is up to 25 centimetres long.*

Foul fact!

If grabbed by the back of the neck, the sun bear can swivel its body around inside its loose neck skin to bite its attacker.

Creepy disguise

Many creepy crawlers are camouflaged so they can hide. Some hide from predators, and others hide so they can catch prey.

▶ *The decorator crab* **camouflages** *itself all over so that predators find it hard to spot.*

▼ *The orchid mantis is a type of praying mantis. It has enlarged leg segments that resemble petals.*

Decorator crab

The decorator crab has small hooks on its back. It uses these to attach bits of seaweed or sponges to itself. The decorations act as camouflage. Sometimes the crab attaches to a sea anemone. Predators, such as small octopuses, are put off attacking, because sea anemones sting.

Flower mantids

Flower mantids are coloured to look like the flowers on which they live. Their camouflage helps them to avoid predators and to catch prey. The mantids sit very still and wait for prey, such as flies, bees, butterflies and moths, to come within reach. Then they pounce. The orchid mantis also eats tiny pieces of banana.

The female Macleay's spectre stick insect can curl her tail over her body like a scorpion.

▶ *If threatened, the Macleay's spectre stick insect sways like a dry leaf blowing in a breeze.*

Macleay's spectre stick insect

The Macleay's spectre stick insect, or giant prickly stick insect, lives in New Guinea and northern Australia. A female can lay thousands of eggs in her lifetime. The eggs can take up to two years to hatch. The newly hatched young, called **nymphs**, resemble ants.

Stinky birds

Some birds are known for causing a real stink! Whether it is the birds themselves, their eggs or the mess they make with their faeces, the smell can be really awful.

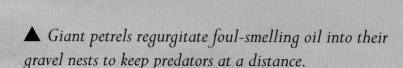

▲ *Giant petrels regurgitate foul-smelling oil into their gravel nests to keep predators at a distance.*

Giant petrels

Northern and southern giant petrels lay stinky eggs. It is believed that the eggs smell to put off predators. Even after 100 years in museum collections, the eggshells still smell. The body of the southern giant petrel has a strong, musky smell, too. It feeds mainly on dead seals and penguins, as well as krill and squid.

Foul fact!

Starling guano is acidic and can damage buildings made of sandstone.

Hoopoes

Hoopoes are found in Europe, Asia and Africa. The hoopoe makes a foul-smelling nest in a hole in a tree trunk or wall. It adds lots of faeces to the nest to put off predators. It also squirts faeces at intruders.

▶ *The Hoopoe eats insects and worms. It has a colourful crest which it raises when excited.*

Starlings

Starlings are very common in Great Britain, where there are about 500,000 breeding pairs. The birds nest in spring, often in walls or attics. This can be a problem for homeowners, as the birds make lots of noise – and produce lots of guano. The faeces are not only smelly, but can also carry diseases.

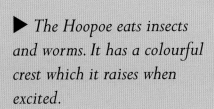

◀ *In winter, thousands of migrant starlings arrive in Great Britain from eastern Europe. They stay there for the winter.*

Tricky tongues

Foul fact!

The sharp, venomous fangs of the diamondback rattlesnake can be more than 2.5 centimetres long.

The tongues of some reptiles are extremely long and sticky. Some have tongues that are V-shaped, and some have brightly coloured tongues that they stick out to scare away predators.

▼ *With incredible speed, a Parson's chameleon shoots its tongue out at an insect on a twig. It can capture prey up to one-and-a-half body lengths away.*

Chameleons

When a chameleon sees prey, such as a grasshopper, cricket or praying mantis, it aims its long, sticky tongue at the animal. As the tip of the chameleon's tongue hits the prey, it forms a cup shape that sticks to the creature and traps it. The chameleon then pulls the insect back into its mouth. Some large chameleons also eat other lizards and small birds.

Diamondback rattlesnakes

The two species of diamondback rattlesnake are North America's most poisonous snakes. They are aggressive, but warn predators of their presence by shaking the rattle at the end of their tail.

▲ *The diamondback rattlesnake has a large, forked tongue which can 'taste' the scent of prey on the air.*

Blue-tongued skinks

Blue-tongued skinks live in Australia and New Guinea. They sleep in leaf litter or fallen logs, and during the day hunt for snails, slugs, insects, spiders, berries, flowers, **fungi** and **carrion**. Although their teeth are not sharp, they can give a powerful bite.

▶ *When alarmed, the blue-tongued skink sticks out its blue tongue to scare away predators.*

117

Slippery skins

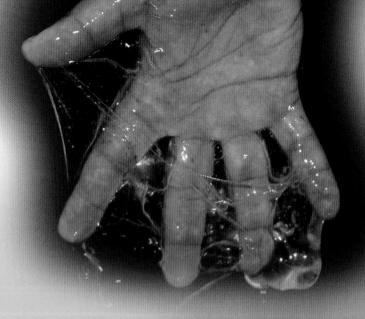

Large slimy creatures can be found both on land and in the water. One of the most unusual is the axolotl. It has the unique ability to regrow parts of its body, including its tail and legs, its heart and its brain cells.

▲ *When slime eels are taken out of the water and handled, they drip with sheets of slime.*

Slime eel

The slime eel is a deep-sea eel from the central north Pacific Ocean. It looks similar to the hagfish (see page 27), and has a slitlike mouth and blunt head. The slime eel is a parasite. It burrows into the bodies of halibut and other big fish.

▼ *Unlike most worm lizards, the Mexican worm lizard, or ajolte, has strong front legs and sharp claws for digging.*

Worm lizards

There are more than 150 species of worm lizard. They look a bit like earthworms, but unlike worms their bodies are covered in scales. Worm lizards live underground. Most species do not have legs – they burrow by pushing the soil with their thick, bony skulls. One species, the Florida worm lizard, lives in sandhills and forests in north and central parts of Florida. It grows to about 30 centimetres long and is about as thick as a pencil.

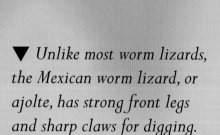

Axolotl

The axolotl lives in only a few freshwater canals near Mexico City. In the wild, it is now an **endangered species**, as its habitat is being destroyed. If its habitat dries up, the axolotl loses its gills and it changes to become a land-living salamander.

▼ *The axolotl has weak eyesight. To find food, it uses its sense of smell and special organs that help it to sense movement.*

Foul fact!

From the 1300s to the 1500s, the Aztec people of Mexico regularly ate axolotls as part of their diet.

Slimy fish

Fish produce slime from their skin. The slime protects them from parasites and diseases and helps them to move through the water. It can also make them taste bad, as well as make them harder to catch.

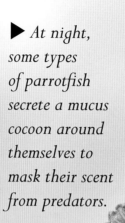

▶ *At night, some types of parrotfish secrete a mucus cocoon around themselves to mask their scent from predators.*

▼ *To get rid of its own slime, the hagfish ties itself in a knot and sweeps the knot towards its head to scrape itself clean.*

Parrotfish

Parrotfish are named after their ridged, parrot-like beak, which they use to scrape algae from coral reefs. The slimy cocoon that they sleep in at night provides good protection from parasites, which suffocate in the slime.

Hagfish

If another fish tries to eat a hagfish, the predator gets a mouthful of slime. When threatened, hagfish ooze out a small amount of thick, white fluid. The fluid absorbs seawater and swells to form a thick, heavy slime. The slime suffocates predators by clogging their gills.

Slimeheads

Slimeheads are commonly known as roughies. They live in the cold, deep waters on the eastern and western edges of the Pacific, the eastern Atlantic, and the seas around Australia and New Zealand. They breed later in life and live longer than most fish, up to 150 years!

▼ *Slimeheads, such as this southern roughy, have a network of slime-filled dents in their head.*

Foul fact!

Slimeheads were renamed orange roughies to tempt people to buy them to eat.

Ugly brutes

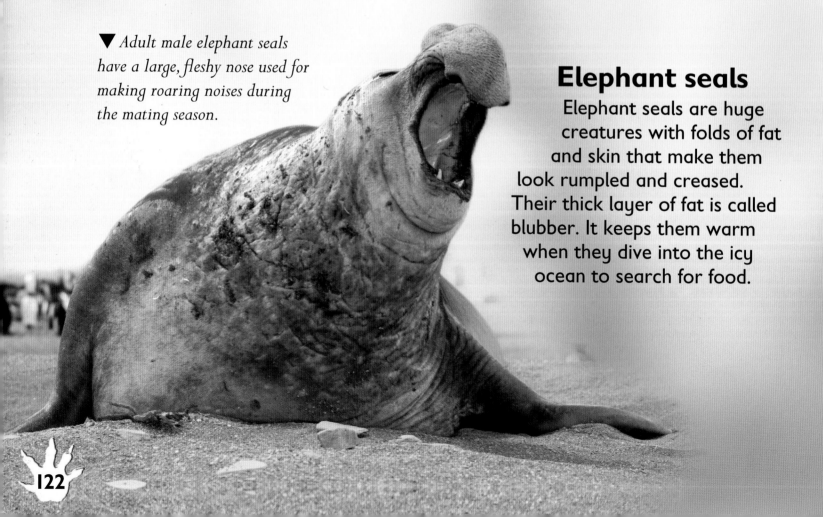

Some animals look ugly. They may have no hair, or have lumps on their faces, or be large and flabby with big noses. Although they look strange, these features are special adaptations that help the animals to survive.

▲ *These naked mole rats are coming out of a tunnel in a zoo. Their small eyes and ears are almost hidden in the folds of their skin.*

Naked mole rat

The naked mole rat lives in long tunnels in the grassy regions of eastern Africa. It lives in groups of 20 to 300 members, ruled over by a queen. Hairless skin means that the mole rat does not overheat in its underground home.

▼ *Adult male elephant seals have a large, fleshy nose used for making roaring noises during the mating season.*

Elephant seals

Elephant seals are huge creatures with folds of fat and skin that make them look rumpled and creased. Their thick layer of fat is called blubber. It keeps them warm when they dive into the icy ocean to search for food.

A warthog's
canine teeth
grow constantly.
It uses them to
dig and search
for food.

▼ *The four hard bumps on
the warthog's face cushion the
blows when it fights.*

Warthog

The warthog belongs
to the pig family. It lives
in Africa. The male
warthog has four hard
bumps on its face that
look like warts – from
which it gets its name.
Males and females have
curved tusks, which
they use as weapons,
growing out of
their mouths.

Pond perils

There are many strange creatures living in ponds, streams and rivers around the world. Some of these **aquatic** creepy crawlers have fierce eating habits.

▶ *Giant water bugs live in ponds and streams in North America, South America and East Asia.*

▼ *A dragonfly larva has hooks on its hinged jaw. It shoots out its lower jaw and stabs its prey with the hooks. Then it tugs the prey back into its mouth.*

Giant water bugs

Giant water bugs prey on small fish, frogs and salamanders. They stab their prey with their sharp 'beak' and inject their saliva into the prey's body. The saliva contains **enzymes** that make the prey's body dissolve, and the bugs suck up the liquid.

Dragonfly larvae

Dragonfly larvae are aggressive underwater predators. They have large eyes, which they use to spot their prey — water bugs, tadpoles and even small fish. The larvae propel themselves through the water by forcing a current of water out of their rear end.

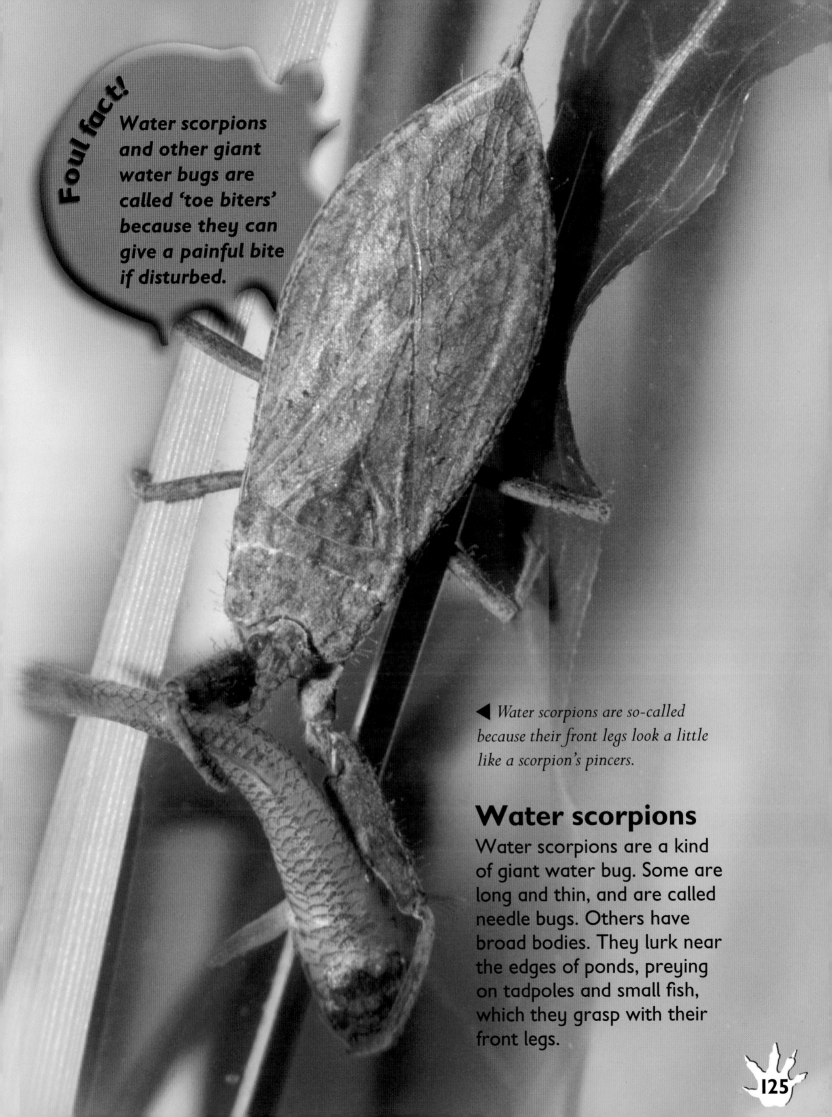

◀ *Water scorpions are so-called because their front legs look a little like a scorpion's pincers.*

Water scorpions

Water scorpions are a kind of giant water bug. Some are long and thin, and are called needle bugs. Others have broad bodies. They lurk near the edges of ponds, preying on tadpoles and small fish, which they grasp with their front legs.

125

Beastly bats

Many bats look very strange. Humans have made up stories about bats being evil because of the way they look. But they actually do a lot of good, eating large numbers of harmful insects.

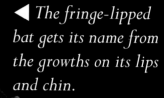
◀ The fringe-lipped bat gets its name from the growths on its lips and chin.

Fringe-lipped bat

The fringe-lipped bat lives in Central and South America. It eats insects, other bats and frogs. Just by listening to the frogs' mating calls, the bat can tell which frogs are poisonous and which are safe to eat.

Wrinkle-faced bat

The wrinkle-faced bat lives from southern Mexico to Venezuela. It has lots of hairless folds of skin on its face. The bat roosts in trees by day. After dusk, it eats fruit such as ripe bananas.

◀ When roosting, the bat pulls up a fold of skin from its chin and hooks it over the top of its head, covering its ears.

Spectral bat

The spectral bat is one of the largest bats in the world. It has a wingspan of up to 1 metre. It is found in southern Mexico, Ecuador, Peru, Brazil, Guyana, Suriname and Trinidad. The spectral bat hunts at night for birds, small mammals, reptiles, frogs, large insects and fruit – and even other bats! Both parents take care of the single baby that is born each year. The father bat often sleeps with both the mother and baby wrapped in its wings.

Foul fact!

A spectral bat suddenly drops from a tree onto its prey as the prey passes below.

▲ The spectral bat has long canine teeth. When it hunts, it drops onto its prey from above.

Tricky travels

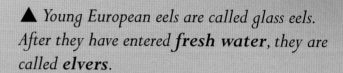

Some fish make incredibly long journeys. They may swim for more than 3000 kilometres – three times the length of Great Britain. Some fish actually walk on land using their fins as legs.

Salmon

Salmon hatch in small streams. After a year, they swim to the ocean, where they live for several years. They then make an extraordinary journey back to the stream where they hatched to **spawn**.

▲ *Young European eels are called glass eels. After they have entered* **fresh water***, they are called* **elvers***.*

European eel

The European eel begins life in the Sargasso Sea, in the North Atlantic. It then swims to Europe or North Africa. Females travel inland along streams and rivers, and live in fresh water for 7 to 15 years. They then return to the Sargasso Sea to lay their eggs and die.

▼ *Scientists believe that salmon use the Sun, Moon and stars to find their way across thousands of kilometres of ocean.*

Mudskippers

Mudskippers can breathe through their skin long enough for them to skip across a muddy area of shore. They can even survive for days out of water as long as they keep their gills wet. Special storage bags behind the eyes hold seawater, which is used to keep the **gill flaps** damp.

▼ *Out of water, a mudskipper uses its fins as legs to push itself along.*

Foul fact!

If a mudskipper dries out, its gills begin to stick together and it cannot breathe.

Gross eaters

Some animals have unpleasant eating habits. They may feast on dead animals, digest the bones of their prey in acid or use their strong jaws to rip their prey apart.

▲ *The wolverine's sharp, powerful claws help it to kill prey such as rabbits.*

Wolverine

The wolverine is sometimes called a skunk bear or glutton. It lives in Alaska, Siberia, northern Canada and Scandinavia. It often eats the remains of animals killed by wolves. It will also kill prey itself, by pouncing on an animal from a tree or rock, tearing it apart.

Pangolins

Pangolins are also called scaly anteaters. They live in tropical Asia and Africa, and are covered with brown scales. The pangolin eats termites, ants and other insects, which it sniffs out and catches on its long, sticky tongue. It has no teeth. Instead, horny plates in its stomach grind down the food before it is digested.

▶ *The pangolin marks its territory by squirting a strong-smelling liquid from glands under its tail.*

Hyenas

Hyenas are strong, doglike creatures that live in Africa and India. Although they **scavenge** and eat carrion (dead animals), they also catch young hippos, gazelles, zebras, wildebeest and antelopes. The stomach of a spotted hyena can hold up to 15 kilograms of meat, so it can go for several days without food.

▶ *The spotted hyena uses its large jaws to crush the bones of its prey and tear through thick skin.*

Foul fact!

Hyenas have strong acid in their stomach. This helps them to digest chunks of meat and even bones.

Terrifying toads

Toads tend to travel further from water than frogs, and their skin is often dry and bumpy, rather than smooth.

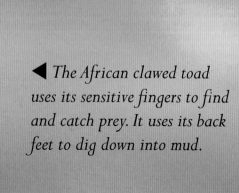

▲ *The female star-fingered toad carries her eggs buried in the skin of her back.*

African clawed toad

The African clawed toad lives in water. It uses its claws to stir up mud to find insects to eat. If the toad's pond dries up, it buries itself in the mud and waits until it rains.

Star-fingered toads

Star-fingered toads, also called Surinam toads, live in the Amazon region of South America. When the female lays her eggs, they stick to her back with slime and gradually sink into her skin. About 12 to 20 weeks later, the babies push their way out of her skin and swim off.

◀ *The African clawed toad uses its sensitive fingers to find and catch prey. It uses its back feet to dig down into mud.*

Giant cane toad

The giant cane toad is from Central and South America. In 1935, it was introduced to Australia to control a beetle that was damaging sugar cane crops. The toad bred quickly, and is now a pest itself. Pets, humans and the **native** animals that prey on frogs and toads all fall victim to its poison.

▼ *The giant cane toad produces a poison from glands on each shoulder. If humans eat the poison, it can cause them to have a heart attack.*

Foul fact!

The largest giant cane toad was 23 centimetres long – the size of a small dog!

Slimy bugs

Some slimy creatures cause problems for humans. Millipedes and froghoppers can do terrible damage to crops. Maggots are useful to fishermen, but their parent flies can carry diseases.

▲ Maggots hatch from flies' eggs. The flies lay their eggs on rotten food and on the bodies of dead animals. This provides the maggots with plenty to eat when they hatch.

Maggots

'Maggot' is the name given to fly larvae. Some types of maggot, such as botfly larvae, are parasites. They live under the skin of living animals, causing sores, cuts and even death. This is a real problem in warm, damp climates.

▼ The spotted snake millipede needs to stay damp and slimy. It is most often found in heavy soils, which are less at risk from drying out.

Foul fact!

Millipedes prefer to live in ground that has been covered in manure, or animal faeces.

Snake millipedes

Snake millipedes live in leaf litter, under bark and in moss. They are common in gardens throughout Britain. Snake millipedes use their 200 legs to climb trees, where they graze on green algae. They sometimes find their way into houses, too.

Froghoppers

Froghoppers are small, brown insects that can jump 70 centimetres through the air to reach the next plant. This is an amazing distance for such a tiny creature. Their larvae are known as **nymphs**. For protection, the nymphs develop inside a blob of froth, called cuckoo spit, often seen on grass. The froth hides the nymph from predators, keeps it damp and stops it from getting too hot or cold.

◀ *A froghopper nymph, or spittlebug, creates its protective froth by blowing air into a fluid excreted from its* **anus***.*

Scary beasts

Frightening myths and superstitions have been created around some animals. But these stories are not true, and it is important to learn about these amazing animals.

Wolves

Wolves live in many northern countries. Grey wolves are fast runners, and chase down their prey. They hunt deer, elk, moose, hares and beavers. In some places wolves kill farm animals and eat rubbish from bins. Wolves live in packs of up to 20 animals. These packs are very close and organized: travelling, hunting and raising families together.

◄ *Wolves have large, sharp teeth which help to tear meat.*

Aye-aye

The aye-aye lives in the rainforests of Madagascar. Using its long, bony middle finger, it taps on tree branches and listens for beetles and grubs moving under the bark. When it hears a grub moving, it picks it out of the bark using its long finger. It also uses its middle finger to scoop out the flesh from inside coconuts.

Foul fact!

Some people in Madagascar believe that a person will die if an aye-aye points its long middle finger at them.

▶ *The aye-aye's **habitat** is the tropical forest. It hunts at night in the trees.*

Amazing adaptors

To help them to survive, some reptiles and amphibians have changed, or adapted, over time to new conditions. In hot, dry places they may live mainly underground away from the heat of the sun, and only come out when it rains.

Water storing frog

The water storing frog lives in Australia. The frog stores water in large quantities in its **bladder** for use in dry periods. In hot conditions, it burrows into the mud and makes an underground hole, or cell. It may sleep there for several years, waiting for cooler, wetter weather to arrive.

Tokay

The tokay is a **gecko**. It has developed special clingy toe pads for gripping. The pads are covered in tiny hairs. The ends of these hairs are split into many parts. These tiny hairs can stick to smooth surfaces. To release its grip, the tokay curls its toes. It lives in South East Asia, north-east India, Bangladesh and New Guinea.

◀ *The water storing frog is only seen after heavy rain. When the male calls, it inflates its throat to make the sound louder.*

Foul fact!

Tokays are aggressive, and when they bite, they do not easily let go.

▲ *The tokay's soft, velvety skin is coloured to help it blend in with tree bark.*

Sirens

Sirens live in the southern United States, in shallow pools and ditches that dry up in warm weather. When their pools dry up, sirens burrow into the mud and make a **cocoon** out of hardened slime and old skin. Large adults can survive in this way, without food, for nearly two years.

▶ *Sirens have a horny, beaklike mouth and a pair of tiny front legs, but no back legs.*

Funky fishing

Some fish have developed unusual ways to catch their prey. They 'go fishing', using a fake fish on the end of a line that is attached to their head.

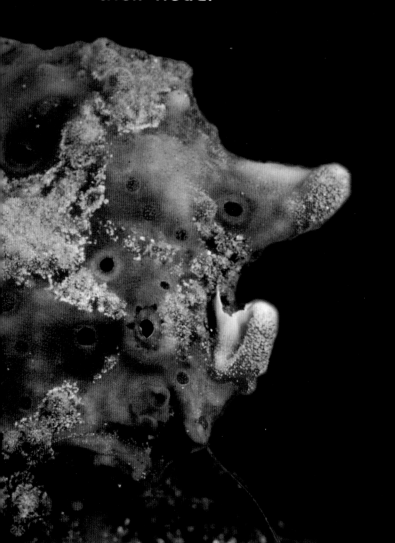

▲ *The gulper eel has a very large, loosely hinged, pouchlike mouth.*

Gulper eel

The gulper eel is also known as the umbrellamouth gulper or pelican eel. Its large mouth allows it to swallow fish much larger than itself. It also has a special organ on the end of its tail that lights up. Scientists think this may help the eel to attract prey.

Warty frogfish

Warty frogfish have a long spine under their mouth, at the end of which is a lure that looks like a small fish. The lure is used to draw prey into close range, so the warty frogfish can snap it up. Warty frogfish are well camouflaged. They can change colour until they match the surrounding sponges or corals.

◄ *A warty frogfish waves its lure in the hope of attracting a prey fish to swim close by.*

▼ *Special light-producing bacteria live inside the lure of the fanfin anglerfish.*

Anglerfish

Anglerfish have a huge mouth and lots of sharp teeth. On the front of their head, they have a long spine with a fleshy lure at the end. Prey see the fleshy lump wriggling and think it is a worm to eat. The jaws of the anglerfish snap shut automatically when a creature touches the **bait**.

Foul fact!

The stomach of an anglerfish is able to stretch to twice its normal size to hold large prey.

Foul fleas

Fleas are tiny creatures, but they cause a lot of trouble. Not only do they bite animals and people, making them itch horribly, but they also carry and spread diseases.

▼ *The human flea also feeds on pigs. It is able to jump higher than the rat flea, as pigs are higher off the ground than rats.*

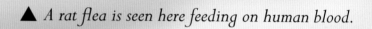

▲ *A rat flea is seen here feeding on human blood.*

Rat flea

The rat flea is a carrier of **bubonic plague**, also known as the Black Death. It can pass this disease to humans. First the flea feeds on a rat that is carrying plague **bacteria**, and takes in the bacteria without being harmed. Then it feeds on a human, passing the bacteria into the person's blood. Bubonic plague is rare today, but over the centuries it has killed many hundreds of millions of people.

Human flea

The human flea is rare today, as it does not like the dry conditions created by central heating. But it used to be very common. In Ancient China, flea traps made from ivory or bamboo were warmed and put into beds to catch the fleas. In 16th-century England, rich ladies wore fur collars known as 'flea cravats' to catch the fleas, which were then shaken out.

Cat flea

The cat flea is the most common type of flea. It is found all over the world. Like other fleas, it feeds on fresh blood. The cat flea bites and sucks the blood of cats, dogs and humans. The bites make small, red bumps on the skin that are extremely itchy. Fleas lay up to one egg an hour. The larvae that hatch develop into adults inside a silk **cocoon**.

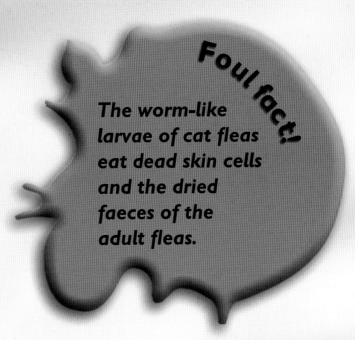

Foul fact!

The worm-like larvae of cat fleas eat dead skin cells and the dried faeces of the adult fleas.

▶ *Fleas can jump 150 times their own length. They jump to move from one host animal to another.*

Poisonous flyers

Some birds have developed an unusual protection against predators. They use poison in their feathers or skin to keep themselves safe from enemies.

▶ *The pitohui may be brightly coloured as a warning to predators that it is poisonous.*

Pitohuis

Pitohuis are songbirds from New Guinea. These birds have high levels of poison in their feathers and skin, and smaller amounts in their bodies. They eat a type of beetle that contains the poison. The poison may protect the birds from predators and **parasites**.

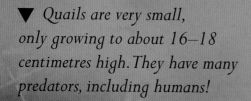

▼ *Quails are very small, only growing to about 16–18 centimetres high. They have many predators, including humans!*

Quails

Some European and **Eurasian** quails are poisonous, but not all of them and not all of the time. People who have eaten quail in northern Algeria, southern France, Greece, north-eastern Turkey and Russia have been known to suffer vomiting, breathing problems, pain and even **paralysis**.

Blue-capped ifrita

The blue-capped ifrita is a small, insect-eating bird found in New Guinea. It eats choresine beetles, which contain a poison. The poison is carried in the bird's blood, and is laid down in its skin and feathers. This protects it from predators.

◀ *The feathers of the blue-capped ifrita are beautiful, but dangerous to touch.*

Foul fact!

The poison in the feathers of ifritas is the same poison as that found in poison-dart frogs.

Super slimers

Of all the slimy animals in the world, the hagfish must be one of the slimiest. Another weird slimer is slime mould, which sometimes behaves like an animal and sometimes like a plant.

▼ *The common mudpuppy has a small range in parts of Canada and the United States. It has moist, slimy skin.*

▲ *Many slime moulds are brightly coloured. They have names such as the dog's vomit slime mould and the scrambled-egg slime mould.*

Slime moulds

Slime moulds are very strange. For part of its life a slime mould looks like a collection of tiny mushrooms or a crusty deposit on a rotting log. When it is reproducing, it turns into a slimy jelly and can creep around.

Common mudpuppy

The common mudpuppy is an amphibian. Most young amphibians lose their gills as they grow and become adults, but the common mudpuppy is different. It keeps it gills and spends its whole life underwater. It prefers to live in shallow lakes or slow-moving streams with rocks to hide under. It eats snails, larvae, worms, small fish and crayfish.

Hagfish

If caught by a predator and held by the tail, hagfish try to escape by secreting quantities of slime from their skin and glands. Hagfish slime includes strong fibres up to 12 centimetres long, similar to spider silk. The fibres are unusual in that they never get tangled. Researchers are trying to find ways of using the fibres to help accident victims and surgery patients, by helping to stop bleeding.

Foul fact!

An adult hagfish can change a bucket of water into slime in a few minutes.

▼ A hagfish produces slime if it is alarmed or disturbed. It may also use slime to deter predators from taking the eggs in its nest.

Create a vampire bat

Create your own vampire bat and hang it from your bedroom ceiling. It will scare off unwanted visitors!

① Trace the half-bat shape below using thin paper or tracing paper. Cut out the shape.

② Fold the black card in half. Clip your tracing paper bat shape to the card. Line up the straight edge of the bat's body with the folded edge of the black card. Cut out the bat shape from the black card and unfold it to reveal a whole bat.

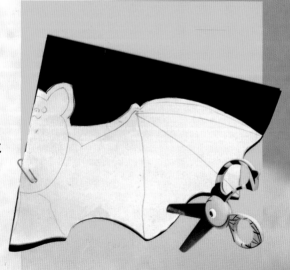

148

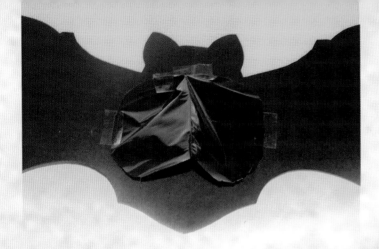

3 Cut out a circle of black plastic from the rubbish bag. Tape the circle to the body, leaving a gap to stuff the body with crumpled newspaper. Stuff and then seal with tape.

4 Glue twigs to the wing shapes to look like the bat's bones.

5 Cut a piece of black card to make a face. Stick the face onto the body as shown. Cut fangs from the white card and stick them to the face. Use glitter glue to make some sparkly eyes.

6 Stick some black thread to your bat and hang it up.

Make a bug

Create your own creepy crawler and watch it scuttle away across the table.

✂ You will need:

A candle
An elastic band
A matchstick
A cocktail stick
A cotton reel

Card
Paint
Glitter glue
Glue

1 Please ask an adult to do all of step 1. Slice off the last 2 centimetres from the end of a candle and remove the wick. Enlarge the hole left by the wick by carefully scraping with a cocktail stick. Cut a groove across one end of the candle.

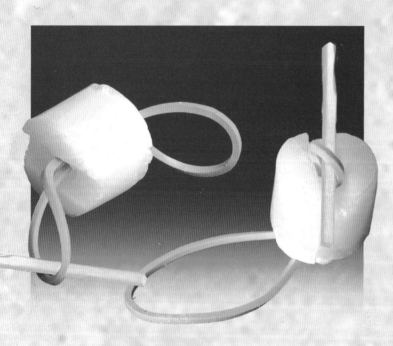

2 Push an elastic band through the piece of candle so it sticks out at both ends. Poke a matchstick through the end of the elastic band and fit it into the groove so that it stays in place.

3 Poke the elastic band through the hole in the middle of the cotton reel. Push half a matchstick through the loop to keep the elastic band in place. Push another matchstick into one of the holes in the cotton reel to stop the half match stick from turning.

4 Your cotton reel creepy crawly is now ready to decorate.

5 Cut out two strips of card or coloured paper. Wind one strip around the cotton reel and stick it in place with glue. Wind the other strip around the candle and stick it in place. Decorate the card with glitter glue. You could make some wings from card and attach them as well.

6 Wind the elastic band by turning the matchstick 'handle'. Let go of the model and watch it 'crawl' or roll away!

Craft a creature

Design an awful animal of your own.

3 Screw up some paper to make the rough shape of your animal's head and body. Wrap sticky tape around the paper so that it holds its shape.

✂ *You will need:*

Paper
Pen
Sticky tape
Rolling pin
Modelling clay

Plastic knife
Large box
Paint
Leaves
Tissue paper
Card
Scissors

4 Use a rolling pin to roll out some modelling clay into a thin layer.

1 Make a list of all the features you would like your animal to have. Does it need slashing claws for digging in sand? How about a long, wobbly tongue for poking into holes to find insects?

2 Draw a sketch of your awful animal to use as a guide.

5 Wrap the modelling clay around the animal's paper head and body. Press the edges of the modelling clay together.

152

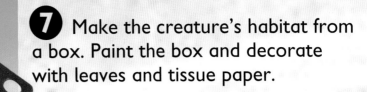

7 Make the creature's habitat from a box. Paint the box and decorate with leaves and tissue paper.

8 On a piece of card, write a display label explaining your animal's lifestyle and appearance, and attach it to the box.

6 From another piece of modelling clay, cut out shapes for the eyes, tongue and any other features, such as scales. Attach these to your model.

Name:
Size:
Weight:
Eats:

Statidraco
2 metres long
70 kilograms
Juicy leaves and fruit, which it
Habitat: picks with its long tongue
Grassland with scattered trees

Glossary

Adapted
Animals that have changed over many generations to suit their living conditions.

Algae
Certain types of plants that grow in or near water. Algae do not have ordinary leaves or roots.

Allergy
Someone who has an allergy is sensitive to certain things, such as pollen or animal hair. Allergic reactions may make a person sneeze or break out in an itchy rash.

Altitude
The altitude of a place is its height above sea level.

Amazon basin
The Amazon basin is the part of South America drained by the Amazon River.

Ambush
To attack something after lying in wait for it to approach or pass nearby.

Amphibians
Animals that can live both on land and in water, such as frogs, toads, newts and salamanders.

Anacondas
Anacondas are large snakes that kill prey animals by crushing them with their body.

Antarctica
Antarctica is the huge, cold continent around the South Pole. It is twice the size of Australia.

Antennae
Long feelers on the heads of insects and crustaceans.

Antifreeze
Antifreeze is a liquid that lowers the temperature at which water freezes.

Anus
The hole in the body from which faeces are pushed out.

Appendage
A body part, such as an arm, leg, tail or fin.

Aquarium
A glass container in which fish and other water creatures and plants are kept. It can also be a type of zoo that you can visit to see many different types of fish and other water creatures in tanks and pools.

Aquatic
'Aqua' means water. Aquatic animals live in water.

Bacteria
Very small organisms that are found everywhere. Some bacteria cause illnesses, such as stomach upsets.

Bait
Bait is the food used to lure creatures so that they may be caught. Fishermen attach bait, such as maggots, to a hook on the end of their line.

Barbel
A barbel is a whisker found on the heads of some fish. Barbels are used as feelers. Some fish use them to find prey.

Biologists
Scientists who study the science of living things, such as plants and animals.

Bladder
The bladder is an organ found in the bodies of humans and animals. It stores urine, which is produced by the kidneys.

Bony fish
A bony fish has a skeleton made of bone. Most fish are bony fish, but some fish, such as sharks, have skeletons made completely of stretchy cartilage.

Bubonic plague
A serious, often fatal, disease caused by bacteria. The disease may be passed from rats to humans by fleas that have lived on infected rats.

Calcium
Bones, teeth and shells are made of calcium, which is a natural material. Calcium is essential for the normal growth and development of most animals and plants.

Camouflage
An animal that is camouflaged is difficult to spot because its patterns or colours blend in with the background.

Carcass
The body of a dead animal.

Carrion
The dead or decaying flesh of an animal.

Cells
Every living thing is made up of many tiny cells. Skin is made up of skin cells, for example.

Cellulose
All plant tissues and fibres are made of cellulose, a material that does not dissolve in water. Cellulose is used to make paper, cellophane, fabrics and even explosives.

Cloud forests
In cloud forests, mist or clouds are found at very low levels. This blocks a lot of the direct sunlight, and the air is very damp. The mist turns into water droplets on the leaves, and these drip to the ground.

Cocoon
A cocoon is a silky pouch spun by the larvae of many insects, such as silkworms and caterpillars. It covers the larva and keeps it safe as it develops into an adult.

Colony
A group of the same kind of animal living together. Insect colonies are usually organized so that every creature has a job to do within the colony.

Crayfish
A lobster-like, freshwater creature.

Crustacean
A type of animal that has a hard outer shell. They live in water, such as crabs, shrimps or lobsters, or on land, such as wood lice.

Cub
The name given to the young of some animals, such as bears, lions and tigers.

Dabbling duck
Shallow-water ducks, including shovelers, that feed by bobbing forward and under the water so as to feed off the bottom.

Decibels
A decibel is a unit used to measure the power of sound. The higher the decibel number, the louder the sound.

Den
Some wild animals make a den or lair in which to sleep, rest or hibernate. They may use a natural hollow in the ground, or may build a den using leaves and branches.

Diabetes
Diabetes is a disease. People with untreated diabetes are unable to control the amount of glucose (a type of sugar) in their blood, and can feel very ill. Diabetes can be controlled with medicines, such as insulin.

Dinosaurs
Dinosaurs were reptiles that became extinct a very long time ago. One of the best known was *Tyrannosaurus rex*.

Disgorge
To force something up from the stomach and out through the mouth.

Dry season
In tropical climates there can be dry and wet seasons. During the wet season rain falls heavily, during the dry season little or no rain falls.

Dysentery
An infection, often caused by bacteria, that leads to severe diarrhoea.

Elver
An elver is a young eel.

Endangered species
An endangered species is in danger of dying out or becoming extinct.

Enzymes
Natural chemicals. They help the bodies of creatures and humans to work properly.

Equatorial
An equatorial region is on or near the equator. The equator is the imaginary line that goes around the Earth at an equal distance from the North and South poles.

Eurasian
Of or relating to Eurasia, the land mass formed by the continents of Europe and Asia.

Extinct
If a species is extinct, it has died out – none of its kind are living.

Extinction
When the last of a species dies, that species is said to be extinct. No more individuals exist.

Eyestalks
Movable stalks with an eye at their tip. They are found in crustaceans, such as crabs, and in some molluscs, such as snails.

Faeces
Waste matter that passes out from an animal's anus.

Fangs
Long, sharp teeth. In a snake, fangs are often hollow and are used to inject venom into their prey.

Ferment
To make a substance change chemically from one state to another. When vegetation ferments inside a bird, it is broken down by living substances, such as yeast or bacteria, into a different state.

Filter-feeding
Filter-feeders are animals that feed by straining or filtering tiny food particles from water. Flamingoes are filter-feeders. They squeeze water out through hairy attachments on their beaks, and eat the food particles that are left behind.

Fresh water
Water that is found in ponds, streams, lakes and rivers. Unlike sea water, fresh water is not salty.

Fungi
Plants without leaves or flowers, such as mushrooms and toadstools. They grow on other plants or decayed material.

Galápagos
The Galápagos Islands are a small group of islands in the Pacific Ocean. They are part of the South American country of Ecuador.

Gastropod
Gastropods include snails and slugs that live on land, water snails and sea slugs. They move by sliding along on their rubbery foot. Most gastropods live in the sea or in rivers and ponds.

Gecko
Geckos are small reptiles. They have toe pads that can stick to smooth surfaces. Some people keep geckos as pets.

Gill flap
When a fish breathes, it takes water in through its mouth. The water passes through the gills, which remove the oxygen from the water. The water is pumped out again through the gill flaps.

Gill rakers
Bony, finger-like sticks found in the gills of some fish. The gill rakers help to support the gills.

Gills
Gills are the organs that help animals that live in water to breathe. The gills take oxygen from the water.

Gizzard
A gizzard is part of the digestive system of some birds, reptiles and fish. It is part of the stomach and has strong, muscular walls used for grinding up food.

Glands
Organs that produce a natural substance for use in the body. Salivary glands produce saliva, for example.

Guano
Guano is the name given to the faeces of birds, bats and seals. It is often used as a fertilizer to help plants grow.

Gulf of California
Part of the Pacific Ocean between the coast of Mexico and the peninsula of Lower California.

Habitat
The natural surroundings of an animal.

Immune
To be protected from, or not affected by, something, such as a disease or poison.

Inflate
To inflate is to get larger, usually by filling with gas. A balloon inflates when you blow into it.

Intestines
Intestines join the stomach and the anus, and help a creature's body to digest food.

Kelp
Kelp is a thick, rubbery type of seaweed that grows quickly. It forms underwater forests in shallow oceans.

Krill
Krill are like tiny shrimps. They are eaten by crabeater seals, baleen whales, manta rays and a few seabirds.

Larva
The newly hatched stage of certain creatures, such as butterflies and ladybirds. Larvae change to become quite different-looking creatures as adults.

Leaf litter
Dead plant material made from decaying leaves, twigs and bark.

Lemmings
Lemmings are small rodents that look similar to hamsters. They live in or near the Arctic, the cold region surrounding the North Pole.

Lichen
A type of dry-looking fungus with many tiny branches. Lichen grows on rocks and trees.

Lure
A lure is something such as an antenna, or strange-shaped tail, which looks like an insect or a worm. It is used by predators to attract creatures that will want to eat the lure, so that they instead may be caught.

Mammal
Mammals are warm-blooded animals with backbones and hair. They produce live young, not eggs. There are around 5400 species of mammals, ranging from the huge blue whale to the tiny bumblebee bat.

Maneater
A large creature that kills a person in an unprovoked attack is described as a maneater. Sharks and tigers, for example, can become maneaters.

Mange
A skin disease in hairy animals, such as dogs, that is caused by a tiny parasitic mite. Animals with mange often lose their hair.

Mangrove swamp
A marine (sea-water) swamp found in tropical or subtropical places.

Metamorphose
When an animal goes through metamorphosis, it changes completely. A caterpillar changes into a butterfly or moth, and a tadpole changes into a frog.

Migrate
When animals migrate, they move from one place to another, usually as the seasons change and food becomes scarce.

Migratory
When animals migrate, they move from one place to another, usually as the seasons change and food becomes scarce.

Mollusc
A mollusc is an animal with a soft body and no supporting bones. Most molluscs, such as snails, have a hard shell to support their body, instead of bones.

Mucus
A slimy substance secreted by the body.

Native
The place where a creature, plant or person originally comes from or was born.

Nectar
Nectar is a sugary liquid produced by plants. Some birds, such as hummingbirds, drink nectar. As they do so, they pollinate the plants that make the nectar, and this enables the plants to produce new seeds.

Nocturnal
Animals that are nocturnal are active at night, when they move around and hunt for food. During the day, they rest and sleep.

Northern hemisphere
The half of the Earth between the North Pole and the equator.

Nymph
The young or larval stage of some animals. Nymphs change into a different form as they become adults.

Organ
A part of the body, such as the heart or liver, that does a special job.

Paralysis
The condition of being unable to move.

Parasite
An organism that lives on or inside another organism, called a host. The parasite feeds off the host.

Photophores
Photophores are light-producing organs found in some deep-sea fish. They produce light in the murky depths of the ocean. The light can act as camouflage for the fish. It may also attract other fish of the same species, or prey.

Phytoplankton
Tiny, free-floating water plants.

Poison-dart frogs
Poison-dart frogs are tiny, colourful, highly poisonous frogs. They are the only animals that can kill a human by touch alone.

Predator
A creature that hunts and kills other animals for food.

Prehistoric
Belonging to very ancient times. Dinosaurs were alive in prehistoric times – the time before recorded history.

Prey
An animal that is hunted and killed for food by another animal.

Protein
A food group needed for growth and the repair of injuries. In some fish, it helps prevent them from freezing.

Quarry
A hunted animal.

Radula
A radula is a mollusc's flexible tongue. It has horny teeth, used for scraping up food.

Rainforest
Dense tropical forests found in areas of very heavy rainfall.

Regurgitate
To bring food back into the mouth after it has been swallowed.

Reptile
Cold-blooded animals that have a backbone and short legs or no legs at all, such as snakes, lizards and crocodiles.

Rice paddies
Flooded fields used for growing rice.

Rodents
A group of animals that includes mice, voles, squirrels and shrews.

Roost
When birds and bats roost, they rest or sleep. A roost is also the place, such as a tree branch, where birds and bats sleep.

Roundworms
Any nematode (a type of worm with a rounded body) that lives in the intestines of humans and other mammals.

Rump
The backside or buttocks of a large animal.

Saliva
The liquid produced in the mouth to keep it moist and to help break down and swallow food.

Salivary glands
Salivary glands are found in the mouth. They make saliva, which is the liquid that we call spit or spittle.

Scavenge
To hunt for and eat dead animals, or carrion. Vultures and hyenas are scavengers. They feed on the bodies of animals that have been killed by predators.

Scavenger
A scavenger hunts for and eats dead animals, or carrion. Vultures and hyenas are scavengers. They feed on the bodies of animals that have been killed by predators.

Secrete
To secrete means to release liquid, especially from glands in the body.

Sewers
Underground pipes and tunnels that carry away sewage from toilets and waste water from households.

Shoal
A large group of fish, usually of the same type, that swim together.

Snout
The projecting nose and mouth of an animal.

Soldier termite
Every termite colony has a large number of soldier termites. They have large mandibles, or jaws, which they use to defend the colony against enemies, usually ants. Some termites also secrete toxic chemicals.

Spawn
The eggs of fish or other water creatures, such as frogs. To spawn is to lay eggs.

Species
A group of animals that share characteristics. Animals of the same species can breed with each other.

Spittle
Saliva that has been spat out.

Spur
A sharp, bony spike on the back of an animal's leg.

Starch
A carbohydrate found in foods such as potatoes, bread and pasta, but also found in paper, textiles and glue.

Subtropical
The regions next to the tropics are called subtropical.

Suction
The act of sucking. Some animals have suction cups on their feet or legs that help them to grip their prey or slippery, steep surfaces.

Tadpoles
The newly hatched young of creatures such as frogs, toads and newts.

Tapeworms
Long, parasitic flatworms that live in the intestines of animals, such as pigs, dogs and humans.

Tapirs
A tapir is a creature with a heavy body and short legs, similar in shape to a pig. It is related to the horse and the rhinoceros.

Tentacle
Tentacles are the long, flexible parts of certain animals, such as jellyfish. They are used for feeling and moving.

Termite mound
Termites construct a nest about one metre below the ground. Above the nest, they pile up the earth into huge mounds full of tunnels, where they live.

Territory
An animal's territory is the area of land that the animal defends against other animals of the same species. Some animals mark the boundary of their territory with scent, and they hunt within that area.

'Third eye'
An organ that detects, or senses, light, found on the head of some reptiles.

Toxin
A poisonous substance, especially one formed in the body.

T-rex
T-rex is short for *Tyrannosaurus rex* – probably the most famous of the large, meat-eating dinosaurs.

Tropical
Tropical relates to the tropics – the area on either side of the equator. The tropics are usually hot and damp.

Tussocks
Clumps or tufts of growing grass.

Typhoid
A serious infectious disease caused by bacteria. It causes headaches, fever and reddish spots all over the body, and can be fatal to humans.

Typhus
A serious infectious disease caused by bacteria passed on by lice and fleas. It causes headaches, fever and reddish spots all over the body, and can be fatal.

Venom
The poison used by some mammals, snakes and spiders to paralyze or kill their prey.

Venomous
A venomous creature uses poison, or venom, to paralyze or kill its prey.

Vermin
Small animals or insects that are harmful and are often difficult to control.

Wading bird
A wading bird is a long-legged shore bird, such as a sandpiper or curlew.

Wetlands
Wetlands are naturally wet areas, such as marshes or swamps. They have spongy soil.

Wingspan
The distance from one wing-tip of a bird or bat to the other.

Worker termite
Within a termite colony the worker termite, which is often blind, is responsible for nest-building and the care of the young.

Worming
When an animal is wormed, it is given a medicine that kills the parasitic worms living in its intestines.

Zooplankton
Animal plankton, made up of small crustaceans and fish larvae.

Index

Copyright © QED Publishing 2009

First published in the UK in 2009 by
QED Publishing, A Quarto Group company
226 City Road, London EC1V 2TT
www.qed-publishing.co.uk

A catalogue record for this book is available from the British Library.

ISBN 978 1 84835 279 7

Printed and bound in China

Author: Lynn Huggins-Cooper
Editing, design and picture research: Starry Dog Books Ltd
Consultant: Sally Morgan

Publisher Steve Evans
Creative Director Zeta Davies
Managing Editor Amanda Askew

Picture credits
Key: t = top, b = bottom, l = left, r = right, c = centre, FC = front cover, BC = back cover.

A = Alamy, BSP = Big Stock Photo.com, C = Corbis, DK = dkimages.com, D = Dreamstime.com, F = Fotolibra, G = Getty Images, HB = Hippocampus Bildarchiv, ISP = iStockphoto, IQM = Imagequest marine, M = Morguefile.com, NPL = Nature Picture Library (naturepl.com), P = Photolibrary, PS = Photoshot, S = Shutterstock.com, SDB = Starry Dog Books, SPL = Science Photo Library.

1 S/ © Patsy A. Jacks; 2–3 S/ © Alex James Bramwell; 3br S/ © Snowleopard1; 4b C/ © Layne Kennedy; 4t S/ © Graham Prentice, 5 S/ © Dmitrijs Mihejevs; 6t S/ © Fukuoka Irina, 7 ISP/ © Harald Bolten, 8b S/ © iDesign; 8t C/ © Craig Aurness, 9 S/ © Philip Date; 10b S/ © Dr Morley Read; 10t S/ © Klaus Nilkens, 11 S/ © Snowleopard1; 12b P/ © Daniel Cox; 12t D/ © Twwphoto, 13 D/ © Alisongoff; 14b C/ © Otto Rogge, 14t S/ © Viorika Prikhodko, 15 C/ © Stuart Westmorland; 16b F/ © David Knowles; 16t G/ © Tim Laman 17 G/ © Roine Magnusson; 18b C/ © Bruce Robison, 18t C/ © Bruce Robison, 19 A/Visual&Written SL / © Mark Conlin/VWPICS; 20b Wikipedia; 20t G/ © Claus Meyer, 21 G/ © Pete Oxford; 22b C/ © Winfried Wisniewski/zefa; 22t ISP/ © Marshall Bruce, 23 / © Peter Johnson; 24b S/ © clearviewstock, 24t S/ © Steve McWilliam, 25 SPL/ Nigel Cattlin/ Holt Studios International; 26b ISP/ © John Pitcher; 26t PL/ © Patti Murray, 27 BSP/ © Katherine Haluska; 28b SPL/ © Fred McConnaughey, 28t ISP/ © Susan Stewart, 29 D/ © Watermark1; 30b D/ © Pixelman; 30t BSP/ © Stuart Elflett, 31 S/ © Fishguy66; 32b A/ © B. G. Wilson

Wildlife; 32t BSP/ © Greg Banks, 33 S/ © Milos Luzanin; 34–35 C/ © Joe McDonald; 35b © Art Segal; 35t ISP/ © Daniel Cardiff, 36b C/ © Arthur Morris; 36t S/ © Olga Bogatyrenko, 37 A/ © Juniors Bildarchiv; 38b P/ © Wells Bert & Babs; 38t © Dr Rafe M. Brown, 39 C/ © Gary Bell/zefa; 40b © Christian Fuchs; 40t A/ © Holt Studios International Ltd, 41 PL/ © Oxford Scientific; 42–43 DK/ Frank Greenaway © Dorling Kindersley; 42t NPL/ © Rod Clarke/ John Downer Productions, 43 C/ © DK Limited; 44b C/ © Michael & Patricia Fogden; 44t PS/ © Jean-Louis Le Moigne/NHPA; 45 ISP/ © Kris Hanke; 46b ISP/ © Susan Flashman; 46t S/ © Michael Ransburg, 47 NPL / © Simon Wagen / J. Downer Product; 48 D/ © Jolka100; 49b C/ © Saed Hindash/Star Ledger; 49c S/ © Dino, 50–51 G/ © Norbert Wu; 50b G/ © Norbert Wu; 51t IQM/ © Peter Herring; 52–53 ISP/ © Jeridu; 52b PL/ © Densey Clyne/Oxford Scientific, 53 BSP/ © Styve Reineck; 54–55 P/ © Oxford Scientific; 54bl © Dominique Weis, UBC, Kilo-Moana cruise, University of Hawaii; 55b P/ © Richard Herrmann; 56b C/ © Nigel J. Dennis/Gallo Images; 56t SPL/ © Rod Planck, 57 G/ © Gavriel Jecan; 58–59 G/ © Roine Magnusson, 58bl S/ © Diego Cervo, 58br M/ sillypieces, 59b C/ © Roger Tidman; 60b PS/ © RoyWaller/NHPA; 60t G/ © Brian J Skerry, 61 C/ © Stuart Westmorland; 62 C/ © Joe McDonald; 63b G/ © Mark Moffett; 63t ISP/ © Bob Kupbens; 64b C/ © Rudolf Kotulán; 64t P/ © Juniors Bildarchiv, 65 S/ © Andy Z; 66–67 National Oceanic and Atmospheric Administration; 66b P/ © Doug Allan; 67 G/ © Norbert Wu; 68–69 G/ © Wolfgang Thieme/dpa; 68b S/ © Snowleopard1, 69b SPL/ © Paul Zahl; 6b ISP/ © Chuck Babbitt; 70b C/ © Stuart Westmorland; 70t D/ © Pufferfishy, 71 G/ © Roger Horrocks; 72b A/ © Bjorn Holland; 72t C/ © B. Borrell Casals; Frank Lane Picture Agency, 73 D/ © Musat; 74b SPL/ © Nicholas Smythe; 74t C/ © Hans Reinhard/zefa, 75 P/ © David M. Dennis; 76b C/ © Markus Botzek/zefa; 76t C/ © Joe McDonald, 77 S/ © Patsy A. Jacks; 78–79 G/ © Gerry Ellis; 78t S/ © Troy Casswell, 79 A/ © blickwinkel; 80–81 BSP/ © Michal Boubin; 80bl A/ © Florian Schulz, 81br A/ © WildPictures; 82b C/ © Norbert Wu; 82t P/ © Max Gibbs, 83 G/ © Norbert Wu; 84b C/ © Theo Allofs; 84t C/ © Joe McDonald, 85 ISP/ © Norman Bateman; 86–87 ISP/ © Paul Tessier; 86bl ISP/ © David T. Gomez, 87tr C/ © Michael & Patricia Fogden; 88b C/ © Hal Beral, 88t HB/ © Juergen Schraml, 89 D/ Dzain; 90b ISP/ © Holger Mette; 90t S/ © Michael Lynch, 91 P/ © M Delpho; 92b S/ © Lori Froeb; 92t C/ © Gary Bell/zefa, 93 ISP/ © Mark Higgins; 94b PL/ © Joe McDonald; 94t G/ Pete Oxford, 95 G/ © Mike Severns; 96 D/ © Fouroaks; 97b S/ © Jorge Pedro Barradas de Casais; 97t A/ © Leslie Garland Picture Library, 98–99b C/ © Michael & Patricia Fogden; 98–99t C/ © Michael & Patricia Fogden, 98bl (inset) D/ © Tonybaggett, 98bl C/ © Tillsonburg; 100t C/ © Michael & Patricia Fogden, 101 C/ © Theo Allofs/zefa, 102b PL/ © Konrad Wothe/Oxford Scientific; 102t A/ © Holt Studios International Ltd, 103 S/ © Dmitrijs Mihejevs; 104b C/ © Joe McDonald; 104t SPL/ Philippe Psaila, 105 C/ © Michael & Patricia Fogden; 106b P/ © Friedemann Koster; 106t F/ © Linda Wright, 107 G/ © Roger Powell/ Foto Natura; 108b P/ © Fredrik Ehrenstrom; 108t G/ © Gary Bell, 109 ISP/ © Dan Schmitt; 110 b P/ © Stan Osolinski; 110t S/ © clearviewstock, 111 S/ © Vova Pomortzeff; 112b C/ © Xenobug; 112t D/ © Pufferfishy, 113 C/ © DK Limited; 114–115 G/ © Eric Rorer; 114bl D/ © Argument; 114t C/ © Kit Kittle, 115 C/ © Hans Dieter Brandl; Frank Lane Picture Agency; 116–117 C/ © Frans Lanting, 117b PS/ © Daniel Heuclin/NHPA; 117t ISP/ © Timothy Martin; 118b C/ © Chris Mattison; Frank Lane Picture Agency, 118t C/ © Brandon D. Cole, 119 SPL/ Claude Nuridsany & Marie Perennou; 120b SPL/ © Tom Mcugh; 120t G/ © Norbert Wu, 121 P/ © Karen Gowlett-Holmes; 122b ISP/ © James Richey; 122t C/ © Wolfgang_Thieme/dpa, 123 ISP/ © Elzbieta Sekowska, 124b A/ © Maximilian Weinzierl; 124t C/ © David A. Northcott, 125 A/ © blickwinkel; 126b Professor Phil Myers; 126t C/ © W. Perry Conway, 127 C/ © Gary Braasch; 128b S/ © J. Helgason; 128t PS/ © LUTRA/NHPA, 129 D/ © Anthonyjhall; 130–131 C/ Michael & Patricia Fogden; Gallo Images; 130t SPL/ © Anna Yu, 131t G / © Timothy Laman; 132b PL/ © Zigmund Leszczynski; 132t PS/ © Kevin Schafer/NHPA, 133 A/ © Mark Bowler Amazon-Images; 134b A/ © Holt Studios International Ltd; 134t S/ © Thomas Mounsey, 135 A/ © blickwinkel; 136 P/ © Michael DeYoung; 137 C/ © Frans Lanting; 138–139 S/ © John Bell; 138bl PS/ © Ken Griffiths/NHPA, 139b C/ © Lynda Richardson; 140b G/ © Chris Newbert; 140t SPL/ © Christian Darkin, 141 P/ © Peter David; 142b PL/ © Paulo De Oliveira/Oxford Scientific; 142t PS/ © George Bernard, 143 SPL/ © Eye of Science; 144b P/ © Juniors Bildarchiv; 144t © Dr John P. Dumbacher, 145 © Dr John P. Dumbacher; 146b PS/ © Daniel Heuclin/NHPA; 146t S/ © Steve McWilliam, 147 C/ © Brandon D. Cole.